LEADERSHIP PRACTICES

A Global and Biblical Perspective

Dr. Widza Bryant
and
Dr. Cedric Bryant

ISBN 978-1-0980-6000-8 (paperback)
ISBN 978-1-0980-6001-5 (digital)

Christian Faith Publishing, Inc.
832 Park Avenue
Meadville, PA 16335
www.christianfaithpublishing.com

Printed in the United States of America

To God first and foremost, for His faithfulness in orchestrating our lives. Over the years, we have tried to change this project many times, and each time, the Holy Spirit steps in to redirect our paths to make this work possible. This project would not have been possible without the promises of Isaiah 40:31: "They that wait upon the Lord, shall renew their strength, they shall mount up with wings of eagles, they shall run and not grow weary, they will run and not be faint." We hope you are as excited to read this manuscript as we were writing this—a combination of both of our doctorate projects.

This manuscript is also dedicated to our five children: Olivier, Vladimir, Ruth, Daniel, and Grace Bryant; to our mothers, Alourdes Cauvin and Ida Y Parker; our late mother, Martha Davis; our spiritual mother and father, Sister Lunise Fortune and Rev. Marc Pean. We love you very much.

CONTENTS

INTRODUCTION

The term leadership has been the dominant trend for decades, and countless definitions have evolved as a result. Winston and Patterson's (2006) search of the Expanded Academic Database in 2003 of published articles using the term "leadership" returned over twenty-six thousand essays. The two explain the quest to define "leadership" by scholars as to the story of the "blind men describing a moving elephant," one that is subject to different interpretations and variations.

Many scholars have dedicated their time in an attempt to invent the most appropriate meaning over the years. Winston and Patterson believe that the quest to pursue the "right" definition of leadership is "perhaps" due to scholars' understanding rooted in social sciences research. They surmise,

> Perhaps our training in research and the exploration in the social sciences caused us to miss the whole as we probed the parts. Social science research often uses reductionism in studying and understanding social phenomena, with studies focusing on relationships among selected variables. This is not a bad thing to do and has helped us understand hundreds, if not thousands, of social science concepts. However, in the case of the study of leadership, this approach has taken us away from the whole. And it is this whole that we seek to understand.

Scholars' interpretations of leadership have led to countless definitions of the term leadership. The Journal of Educational and

Social Research (2016, vol. 6, no. 2) summarizes some of the interpretations of leadership as follows: "Leadership is a process whereby an individual influence a group of individuals to achieve a common goal" (Northouse 2010, 3); leadership is a process whereby intentional influence is exerted over other people to guide, structure and facilitate activities and relationships in a group or organization (Yukl 2010, 21); leadership is both a necessary process and a specialized role held by an individual (Tafvelin 2013).

Moreover, Zeitchik (2012) believes that leadership means to motivate the members of a team to do their best; to inspire others to pursue their targets based on the parameters set. Kruse (2013) defined leadership as a process of social influence, which maximizes the efforts of others toward the achievement of a goal. Matei and Vazquez-Burguete (2012) describe leadership as the process of "articulating visions, embodying values, and creating the environment within which things can be accomplished." According to Bush (2003), three dimensions form the basis of his definition of leadership: leadership as influence, leadership and values, and leadership and vision. Some scholars see leaders as servants. In this line, Crippen (2005) points out that the primary purpose of servant leaders is to help rather than lead. Bijur (2000) believes that "leadership means enhancing human potential—creating the right environment for people to develop their abilities."

Northouse (2013) expounds there are as many different definitions of leadership as there are people who have tried to define the term. He affirms that "the public has become increasingly captivated by the idea of leadership, and scholars continue to have opposing views of what constitutes leadership" (p. 1). He adds that "leadership over the years has changed and continues to evolve" and that "putting a definition to the term has proved to be a challenging endeavor for scholars and practitioners alike." He believes that the term leadership has spanned over decades, beginning with leadership as power-positioned, personality traits, behavioral-leaning, group process, and into the twenty-first-century agreement between scholars that the term leadership is too complex of a concept, one that will continue to have different meanings for different people.

Despite the work by many over the years to define leadership in ways consistent to God's intended purposes, misrepresentative applications, variation in viewpoints often overshadow its originality resulting in continued quests to harmonizing leadership definition, intent, and practices. It is fair to conclude that leadership is inherently a part of everyone's lives. "Leaders reside in every city and country, every position and place. Leaders are employees and volunteers, young and old, rich and poor, male and female. Leadership knows no racial or religious bounds, no ethnic or cultural borders; there are as many as two hundred definitions of leadership over the years with a new paradigm every decade" (Kouzes et al. 2004). Hence and Kuhn (2012) deduce that "theories exist because study of both science and leadership is not static. It is exposed to different interpretations and ongoing studies by all groups of scholars and practitioners alike."

Could the inexorable pursuits to define leadership and align its practices be the cause of man's biased predispositions from God's intended purpose? A trend that commenced before humanity even existed—"the rebellion of Lucifer" against God, as summarized in Isaiah 14:12–15:

> How you have fallen from heaven, O morning star, son of the dawn! You have been cast down to the earth, you who once laid low the nations! You said in your heart; I will ascend to heaven; I will raise my throne above the stars of God; I will sit enthroned on the mount of assembly, on the utmost heights of the sacred mountain. I will make myself like the Most-High. But you are brought down to the grave, to the depths of the pit.

Humanity is impacted due to the one-sided nature of our understanding of leadership as influenced by dominance for most of the earth's history" (Stanley 2017) with Adam and Eve's disobedience in conjunction with Satan's efficacious effort to turn them (Adam and Eve) away from the will of God. Humanity's mockery to God's purpose continues throughout biblical history, which often leads to harmful consequences. The narrative of Matthew 20:20–24 reveals the degree to which even Jesus's disciples were impacted by self-ascendant and dominance tendencies. "The mother of James and John sought to persuade Jesus to honor her sons with high positions in his kingdom, and the jealousy and anger among the other disciples reveal that unhealthy ambition lurked just below the surface among them" (Stanley 2017). Glaring evidence of the quest for self-seeking glory dominated biblical stories and continues to be detrimental today in leadership practices.

Upon creation, God created a global world that mandated a global leadership approach as corroborated in Genesis 1:28. God expected His creation (man) to be like Him and to take complete dominance in collaboration with one another. He gave us His attributes and the mental capacity (*A Global Mindset*) to enable us to work across culture with no boundaries or border limitation, to be "fruitful and multiply," to be inclusive and accessible in our approach.

Chapter 1
In the Beginning God Created Leaders for Good Works

The concept of leadership birthed in the Garden according to Genesis succeeding creation of all things and sufficient resources. In Genesis 2:1–18, we glean that humanity was given leadership over creation and was intended to thrive under man's leadership (Phillips 2016):

> The heavens and the earth were completed in all their vast array...The Lord God made all kinds of trees grow out of the ground—trees that were pleasing to the eye and good for food. In the middle of the garden were the tree of life and the tree of the knowledge of good and evil...The Lord God took the man and put him in the Garden of Eden to work it and take care of it. And the Lord God commanded the man, "You are free to eat from any tree in the garden; but you must not eat from the tree of the knowledge of good and evil, for when you earth from it you will certainly die." (Genesis 2:1–18)

The biblical definition of the term leadership was established in the sixth day of creation when God said, "Let us make man in our image, in our likeness, and let them rule over all creatures" (Phillips 2016). So God created man in His image; in the image of God, He created him; male and female He created them. God blessed them and said to them, "Be fruitful and increase in number; fill the earth and subdue it. Rule over [every living creature]." Male and female are created in the image of God and given the task of ruling. Bearing the image of God is to represent the authority of God. We serve as vice-regents over creation.

Man was created to do "good" work and to rule in the image of God, using established principles as fundamental elements of leadership. "For we are His workmanship, created in Christ Jesus for good works, which God prepared beforehand that we should walk in them" (Ephesians 2:10). It is essential to understand the applicability of "good works" in this context, unlike the views of many denominations about "good works" as inherent to salvation. The concept "good works" in this context is with the fulfillment of a person's accomplishment concerning his/her career performance. For example, in Genesis 1, we see the expression of satisfaction by God following the completion of the sixth day of work. Those same principles are not only fundamental to the concept of leadership, but they also encompass a globalized and inclusive facet of God's purpose for leaders as captured in Revelation 7:9:

> After this, I looked, and there before me was a great multitude that no one could count, from every nation, tribe, people and language, standing before the throne and before the Lamb. They were wearing white robes and were holding palm branches in their hands. And they cried out in a loud voice: Salvation belongs to our God, who sits on the throne, and to the Lamb.

John's vision of the many assemblies around the heavenly throne depicts an omni-ethnic gathering—one from which no people group on the earth is missing. And one that Jesus demands His church (in Matthew 28) actualize by strategically relocating from among her ranks to proclaim the Gospel (Wells 2018): "go and make disciples of all nations." The last message of Jesus was not just an intentional global charge that required the leaders' strategic movement from one location to another to make disciples among *all* people. It also necessitated proactive actions to reach those who are shunned by society due to various factors, such as accessibility and other impairments.

The command for leadership from God is to be interactive, inclusive, and accessible to all people and nations. Such is only possible through full obedience to the original intent of the mandate and unblemished leadership characteristics (garden principles) that accelerate the capacity for leaders to be a positive force so to withstand the challenges that come with leading others successfully and productively.

There is also the need for leaders to build consensus through trust and interdependent relationships. Such is glaring throughout the Bible—in particular in Genesis—and is evident in the interactions between God and Adam pre-fall. From the biblical account, one can conclude that God was in a close relationship with Adam and Eve. It wasn't unusual for God to visit the first family "in the garden in the cool of the day…" (Genesis 3:8). God's desire to commune with His humankind, despite the sin Adam and Eve committed, was in the prime display when He pronounced judgment against them and the serpent for their disobedience. He, at the same token, extended grace for redemption to restore His relationship with man: "…and I will put enmity between thee and the woman, and between thy seed and her seed: he shall bruise thy head, and thou shalt bruise his heel."

Ever since the fall, God continues to utilize different approaches with man in a quest to maintain a relationship that emphasizes His purpose to "be fruitful and increase in number; fill the earth and subdue it. Rule over the fish in the sea and the birth in the sky and over every living creature that moves on the ground." Nevertheless, man's inability to obey often leads to disappointments that necessitate the need for intervention beginning with the Great Flood. God intervened as a result of man's behaviors, which He described as "wickedness that was great in the earth …that the imagination of the thoughts of man was only evil continually" (Genesis 6:5–6). He consequently began anew and destroyed the entire human race as

He "grieved in His heart and regretted ever made man on the earth." Further, God would confront the disobedience of man at Babel, which caused Him to "come down and confounded their language," to hinder their creativities: "that they may not understand one another's speech …and scattered them abroad from thence upon the face of all the earth" (Genesis 11:7–8).

Leaders are called to enjoy work. The enjoyment of work, according to Genesis, is what would cause "creation" to thrive, resulting in the expansion of resources. Such a concept requires the ongoing need for leaders to align with God's purpose in the course of leading and choosing a vocation, leading others, either in secular or spiritual settings, imitating the attributes on display during creation.

Leadership and Trust

As a role model, a leader can only be successful in a culture that builds on trust, honesty, and role-modeling. It is commonly understood that trust is the foundation of effective relationships that leads to business results (Reina et al. 2017). Trust in the values every day, and in every action, leaders take to create open communication that begins from what leaders say, to how they listen, and how they act on what they learn (Stephenson 2004). Teamwork and collaboration can only happen when people can trust one another. The ability to create shared values that consequently lead to the creation of trust in the leadership's capabilities is not to be ignored. Many times, leaders tend to assume that people will accept their values and do what they say automatically. However, leaders must "lay the foundation of trust before people can individually do their best. Trust is built when we make ourselves vulnerable to other people whose subsequent behavior we cannot control" (Kouzes and Posner et al. 2004). Successively, "leaders will never be able to develop teams to their full potential unless they create an environment of trust." A study by Hay (2002) found that "trust between team members was fundamental to the functioning of the team and saliently promoted cooperative behavior; and that effective team performance is dependent on the formation of trust (Hakanen et al. 2015).

Trust Defined

Rousseau et al. (1998) define trust as a complex phenomenon that enables cooperative behavior, reduces harmful conflict, decreases transaction costs, and promotes effective responses to the crisis. Accordingly, Kadefors (2004), Rousseau et al. (1998) reference three primary forms of trust:

1. Calculus-based trust is when the trustor (the trusting party) perceives that an action that is going to be performed is beneficial to him or her. In this kind of trust, individuals are motivated primarily by economic self-interest;
2. Relational trust appears between individuals who repeatedly interact over time; and
3. In institution-based trust, trust refers to the role of the institution in shaping the conditions necessary to create trust.

Trust is developed when leaders adhere to the truth no matter the consequence. He or she not only tells the truth but also demands that others do the same through sound, fair, and consistent accountability. Ephesians 4:25 teaches, "Therefore, having put away falsehood, let each one of you speak the truth with his neighbor, for we are members of one body." The Bible goes even more profound, referring to truth-tellers as "children of light, and not of the devil," therefore, is considered an abomination to God (Proverbs 6:16–19). Trust is so vital that companies invest a considerable amount of funds on client satisfaction surveys to gather feedback. Most importantly, feedback typically around clients' level of trust in their products or services. For example, the US automaker that suppliers scored lowest in trust spend roughly 50 percent of face-to-face time negotiating price or assigning blame for problems, as opposed to the automaker scoring highest in trust, where only 25 percent of the time spent was on these relatively unproductive activities (Hart and Johnson 1999).

Leaders who tell the truth demonstrate great courage to take a stand and to model the way in typifying their beliefs and their values—upholding policy guidelines regardless of personal interests at a time when it isn't straightforward to do so. In the words of Kouzes and Posner (2012), those leaders generally articulate their beliefs by (a) clarifying values and (b) set an example by aligning actions with shared values. "They stand up for their beliefs. They practice what they preach. They show others by their actions that they live by the values they profess. They also ensure that others adhere to the values that have been agreed on."

Trust also takes time to develop. It does not happen overnight. It requires a personal commitment to learning from others to inspire those who come from other sets of values and traditions to participate with you in building a community of trust (Lingenfelter 2008). One that transcends all odds and challenges. When trust is present, people step forward and do their best to work together efficiently. They align around a common purpose, take risks, think out of the box, and communicate openly and honestly. Conversely, when trust is compromised, people become withdrawn and disengaged. Their confidence in themselves and others erodes, along with their commitment to their work (Reina et al. 2017).

Trust is difficult to build and easy to lose. Because of its complexity, leaders may find it at times difficult to apply a consistent approach to their day-to-day actions. The Center for Creative Leadership suggests that outcomes (in three areas) can be used to measure team effectiveness around trust. The center refers to such as the "Reina Dimensions of Trust, or The Three Cs with three dimensions and sixteen behaviors that provide a practical, behavioral-based framework that helps people raise their awareness of trust" (Reina et al. 2017).

Leadership as a Reciprocal Relationship

"Do unto others as you would have them do unto you" is referred to as the "Golden Rule." It is a command based on the words of Jesus in the Sermon of the Mount. The sermon is parallel to what leaders must do to gain consensus. A leader-follower relationship that is reciprocal has the propensity to bear much "fruit," as opposed to one that is not. A reciprocal link is a follower-centered leadership theory associated with Robert Greenleaf, who became one of the most prominent scholars for introducing the servant leadership theory, which emphasizes that leaders must be attentive to the concerns of their followers and must nurture them. He inferred that servant leaders must put followers first, empower them, and help them develop their full personal capacities (Northouse 2013).

During the last decades, there have been many books and articles on leadership dedicated to the concept of followership. However, the most talked-about work on followership is that of Kelley (1998). Kelley described the ideal follower as participating in a joint process of achieving some common purpose. He ascribed to "effective followers" an array of positive qualities, such as being self-motivated, independent problem solvers, and committed to the group and organization (p. 144).

After decades of nullifying the concept of followership, Weber (1992) affirms that leadership "does not exist in isolation (p. 43). He argues that leaders' successes depend heavily on the reciprocal relationship between leaders and followers. A relationship defined as collaborative leadership that is an influence relationship among leaders and collaborators who intend significant changes that reflect their mutual interest (Rost 2008).

During the last decades, scholars began to dedicate time, constructing a voice for the concept of followership. As a result, it has made increasing headway into the mainstream, and the amount of interest in the topic seems to be escalating. It is becoming part of the organizational vocabulary. Kelley (1998) recognizes that it is rare for someone to talk about leadership without also discussing the similar role of followership. He further states that most leadership courses now have a section devoted to followership. And followership is increasingly taught as a stand-alone course in universities and corporations (pp. 5–6).

He synthesizes followership into five basic styles:

1. *The sheep.* Sheep is passive and looks to the leader to do the thinking for them and to motivate them.
2. *The yes-people.* Yes-people is positive, always on the leader's side, but still looking to the leader for thinking, direction,

vision. If the leader asks them to do something, they've got the energy, and they'll go forward with it.

3. *The alienated.* Alienated followers think for themselves but have a lot of negative energy. Every time the leader or organization tries to move forward, these are the ones who have ten reasons why the leader or organization shouldn't. They are not coming up with the next solution but are skeptical, cynical about the current plan of action.

4. *The pragmatics.* Pragmatics sit on the fence and see which way the wind blows. Once they see where things are headed, they'll get on board. They'll never be the first on board, but they will never let the leader or organization leave without them.

5. *The star followers.* Star followers think for themselves, are very active, and have very positive energy. They do not accept the leader's decision without their independent evaluation of its soundness. If they agree with the leader, they give full support. If they disagree, they challenge the leader, offering constructive alternatives that will help the leader and organization get where they want to go (pp. 7–8).

It is essential, though, to acknowledge that God's formula for leadership success is not static. According to Kuhn (2012), leadership "is exposed to different interpretations and ongoing studies by all groups of scholars or practitioners. Just as there are no common standards in science, its incommensurable with new prototypes that develop incessantly, trigger other prospects for new standards and new interpretations." Finding alignment in approaches to build prosperous, inclusive, and accessible leadership practices ought to be the prime focus for all leaders, may it be secular or spiritual leadership. After all, God established and typified the reciprocal relationship with Adam during creation in the naming of the animals of the earth (Genesis 2:20). In this exchange, the Lord God demonstrated that leaders and followers are bound together in an interdependent manner to accomplish a common purpose.

CHAPTER 2
The Garden Values

I have always been fascinated with the account of Creation, in particular, Genesis 1:2: "Now the earth was formless and empty, darkness was over the surface of the deep, and the Spirit of God was hovering over the waters." This scene where shapelessness darkness and emptiness jumped out because I believe it represents a setting, place organization where ineffective leadership is the order of the day. Leadership without a clear vision is the epitome of darkness, emptiness, and formless.

The account of Genesis helps to understand that leadership and biblical values are intertwined. Leaders and followers' goals realizations are contingent upon one's ability to hold firm the values of creation. God spoke to the disordered state of the formless and empty earth; it instantly transmuted into an orderly state. Those values, according to Genesis, serve as the glue that holds all together. Satisfaction and meaning are generated through these fundamentals of leadership: communication, appreciation for work, global ethical impact, patience, love, equality, and alignment. Humankind was created "in His image and for His glory" and was given akin attributes to follow in His footsteps in replicating His standards for success. The foundation of biblical leadership can be surmised as an approach that conceptualizes leadership on the above-listed principles. Those standards are at the core of all successful interactions among people and entities, be it Christian and non-Christian alike. They are godly values that are considered foundational elements of character. Rue (2001) defines values as "the essence of who we are as human beings."

He explains that our "values get us out of bed every morning, help us select the work we do, the company we keep, the relationships we build, and, ultimately, the groups and organizations we lead. Our values influence every decision and move we make, even to the point of how we choose to make our decisions" (p. 1). They don't change. According to Castillo et al. (2018), "Values reflect what is important to people, and they are organized in a personal hierarchy of importance. Each person has his/her hierarchy, and what is important for one person may be not important for another."

Hultman (2002) defines values as the "standards of importance that guide our process of deciding" (p. 44). It help shape decisions, actions, and, most importantly, beliefs about what is significant. Values help shape a person's reality and actions. Whether positive or negative, he cited, a person's values have a powerful impact on his/her decision-making (p. 44).

Talwar (2009) suggests, "Human values help individual employees and other stakeholders to unleash their capabilities and unearth the latent potential of the organization. It eliminate many troubles and social problems and lead to ethical ways of governance in the organization's culture, policies, systems, and actions; which ultimately will lead to total transformation of the corporate world and provide prosperity and better quality of life for society at large" (p. 43). Global leaders have a moral responsibility to embrace values that apply to different cultures and societies and create opportunities for all.

A. Communication

Communication is the start of all: "in the beginning was the Word," according to John 1:1. By the Word, all things were created. The "Word" produced stability and structure in what is described as a "formless, empty, and dark surface," according to Genesis. By the power of the "Word," what was created on the surface was measured as "good." In order words, "excellence" in how work is performed is contingent upon a leader's ability to communicate for tangible results. Hackman and Johnson (2013) assert that "leadership is first, and foremost, a communication-based activity. For leaders, spend ample time-sharing messages that are then presented to a variety of follower, constituent, and stakeholder groups." Hackman and Johnson also believe that leadership effectiveness depends on our willingness to interact with others and on developing practical communication skills.

God considers communication to be the channel that binds people together. He informs us about good and bad communication in Proverbs 18:21, "Death and life are in the power of the tongue, and those who love it will eat its fruit." Leaders can encourage, strengthen and help others with their speeches, to affirm values and goals, and to improve personal and professional relationships. However, leaders also can discourage and, in some cases, crush others with their speeches as well (Green 2009). Collins (2019) reflects on the basis for effective communication. He stresses that "admitting what God communicates to man is the true basis for effective human communication is often difficult, but the sooner we learn humility on this subject, the sooner we can begin to practice divinely powerful spiritual communication."

In Genesis, God spoke *all* things into being. He transforms and shapes all things through communication. We initiate changes and restore brokenness when we communicate and "verbally" confess our needs and desires to receive His invitation.

We read in Revelation 3:20 that Jesus will enter our lives only *after* we respond to His call—not before: "Behold, I stand at the door, and knock: if any man hears my voice, and open the door (respond to my call), I will come into him and will sup with him, and he with Me." Communication is inherent in and synonymous with leadership. Both are considered intertwined—for there is no leadership without communication. Communication is what brings alignment of thoughts. Regardless of its form, a leader's capacity to communicate effectively is essential to his/her success. Also, leadership communication is particularly important when it is used to unite people from different cultures, values, and backgrounds that make up an organization. Following the "Great Flood," the Lord God blessed Noah and his sons, instructed them to "be Fruitful and increase in number and fill the earth," according to Genesis 9:1. Noah and his family were to fill the earth, to create their reality through their use of communication. God expected Noah to communicate the values with excellence and to follow the rules (ethics). However, the account of what transpired was nothing but contrary to established "garden" leadership values. The people rejected the rules "ethics" for success and embraced their own set of rules, which is outlined in Genesis 11:2: "As the people moved eastward, they found a plain in Shinar and settled there. They said to each other, 'Come, let's make bricks and bake them thoroughly...Come let us build ourselves a city, with a tower that reaches to the heavens, so that we may make a name for ourselves; otherwise, we will be scattered over the face of the whole earth'" which is the instructions God had given for success.

Successful leadership is contingent not just on the leader's ability to communicate effectively, but a follower's disposition to follow the rules (ethics) that are prescribed as well. A leader has the potential to be successful using unethical guidelines through effective communication. For example, Noah and his family members had proven to be very efficient and ingenious in their abilities to communicate their vision not to follow God's prescribed mandate for man to populate the earth; to a vision "to build a city, with a tower that reaches to the heavens, so that we may make a name for ourselves; otherwise, we will be scattered over the face of the whole earth" (Genesis 11:4). The quality of the communication among them resulted in the creation of a shared objective that ultimately lead to goal attainment. The success of their initiative was evident to God. As a result, He set out to impede their efforts in the account of Genesis 11:6: "If as one people speaking the same language they have begun to do this, then nothing they plan to do will be impossible for them."

Leaders are creative and inspiring beings, and communication is the channel that makes all that happen. Hackman and Johnson (2013) assert that "leadership effectiveness depends on our willingness to interact with others and on developing effective communication skills. Those who engage in skillful communication are more likely to influence others" (p. 22). Whether leaders use skillful communication to influence in alignment with organizational goals and objectives or for selfish motives, it has the propensity to transmit values associated with the leader's communication successfully.

The last sixty years have documented as many as sixty-five different classifications of leadership, accentuating the reciprocity behavior between two individuals (Northouse 2013). Such belief has emerged in the last few decades to include several persevering themes such as: (1) do as the leader wishes; (2) influence; (3) traits; and (4) transformation—phenomena that continue to evolve among scholars and researchers to date. The prowess to influence others through effective communication is imperative for leaders. It is one of the characteristics that separate successful organizations from unsuccessful ones.

Dynamic and effective leadership are those that master the art of communication and human relations to work harmoniously with diverse groups, regardless of ethnicity and cultural background. For this reason, technical skills and abilities alone are not sufficient to ensure organizational success. Kouzes and Posner (2012) affirm that technical expertise and "practices are empty without an understanding of the fundamental human aspirations that connect leaders and constituents" (p. 33). Leaders are to demonstrate high competencies and attributes in areas, such as (1) emotional, (2) social, and (3) interpersonal intelligence to be able to build, sustain, and to respond to the expectations of the people they lead. Leaders that are equipped with those skills are capable of building winning teams that are energized to accomplish well-articulated vision and building trust that translates to results and productivity.

Communication Helps to Build Trust and Credibility

Communication brings alignment between leaders and followers and is the mantra for a good partnership. Leaders and followers are in a "partnership" exchange that requires constructive behaviors—where leaders motivate and inspire employees to accomplish goals. One of the reasons why leaders communicate is to build a relationship and establish trust. Communication defines all outcome, whether positive or negative. The effectiveness of the message, i.e., delivery and consequent receipt, ultimately "create a bond of trust between leader and followers…that drives results and enable leader and followers to work together more efficiently" (Baldoni 2003).

God is a communicator who created humankind directly to "commune" with Him. Man was not created to "live" alone. For the Lord God said, "It is not good for the Man to be alone. I will make a helper suitable for him." He created "a helper suitable for Adam" (Genesis 2:18) and ordered them to "work" the land. Our ability to use words to build relationships, to help, and to encourage others in need is inherently part of God's ultimate plan. There are many instances in the Bible that support the value of communication in leadership exchanges. Jethro was able to use words of wisdom to communicate to his son-in-law, Moses, during his visit to the "wilderness." He carefully listened to Moses and responded with grace and wisdom that "the work is too heavy for you; you cannot handle it alone" (Exodus 18:18). Moses did what Jethro told him, and it enabled him to succeed in his assignment (McElmore 2016).

God ordained "men to lead" right from the garden as summarized in Genesis 2:19–20 when He assigned Adam the first leadership task to name the animals: "Now the Lord God had formed out of the ground all the wild animals and all the birds in the sky…He brought them to the Man to see what he would name them; and whatever the man called each living creature, that was its name. So, the Man gave names to all the livestock, the birds in the sky, and all the wild animals."

In the New Testament, we are introduced to Jesus as the greatest Communicator the world has ever seen—the "Word" Himself, according to John 1:1: "In the beginning was the 'Word,' the Word was with God, and the Word was God." And in Matthew 12:37, we are cautioned, "for by your words, you will be justified, and by your words, you will be condemned." Your team, your stakeholders, and society will measure your success on your ability to connect, exchange ideas through communications, or what Baldoni (2003) refers to as "leadership communications." He further explains that communication is similar to "currency" without which a leader is bankrupt.

The ability for leaders to build a relationship is contingent upon his/her capacity to build trust by creating an environment where people are free to provide feedback and address personal and work-related issues through open door communication and reciprocity. They also build trust by "demonstrating leadership in thought, word, and deed (Baldoni 2003).

Components of Communication

According to Kouzes and Posner (2003), "We trust people we know. Therefore, earning trust requires leaders to be accessible to their constituents. Actions such as listening and talking to people, having a consistent physical presence in the workplace, and allowing people to get to know them, require leaders to take risks. It is this willingness to risk—to become known—that provides the foundation for authentic, caring relationships between leaders and constituents. Trust grows out of these relationships."

Communication and Emotional Intelligence

Communication is the glue to everyday exchanges. Relationship successes and failures are all connected to one's ability to communicate effectively. Similar to the concept of leadership, scholars have struggled to define communication relentlessly for decades; but despite this, there is no consensus on a single definition of communication (Littlejohn and Foss 2008). There is, however, agreement on the significance of communication to relationships and organizational successes.

In the story of Babel, the Lord God triggered communication among the people to be unrecognizable as a punishment for disobedience. As ordered by God in the garden and following the Great Flood, the entire world was to be populated per Genesis 1:28, and in Genesis 9:1, Adam, Noah, and his sons were commanded to "be fruitful, to increase in number, and to fill the earth" respectively. Nevertheless, the vision God gave them was overshadowed by "antibodies" and became "discretionary." Such is what occurs when leaders fail to communicate directly to keep the vision alive among stakeholders. Too often, ongoing communication does not seem as important. The assumption is made that people know what is expected of them and, therefore, do not need to be "babysit."

Many organizations face similar challenges among their teams when leaders don't communicate often or communicate effectively. As in the story of Babel, "self-reliance" and unrealistic perceptions of the team's needs often result in inconsistencies of organizational goals and objectives. It is understood after God confounded the language of those in Babel, only small groups could understand one another. They chose to move to other areas of the world… and the remainder of what occurred afterward was evident.

"For generations, the people would have a visible reminder of their foolishness: A great temple tower that had remained a torso or had fallen into decay would stimulate the imagination profoundly. The confusion of languages ultimately had more adverse long-term results. The loss of a common language opened up the world to conflict. For not only did the break-up of language meant the introduction of linguistic differences, but also, the division into different languages meant that we lost our ability to communicate with each other and, in the absence of such communications, antagonisms emerged" (Oster 1996).

The ongoing reminder of organizational and team's vision is as important as assessing and evaluating financials. Communication is the channel that helps to keep the vision alive and shared.

Leaders are mandated to communicate and to build support for the direction in which organizations take; therefore, everyone has to fervently believe in and commit to a common purpose (Kouzes and Posner 2012).

Biblically speaking, when Joshua was about to lead the people of God into the promised land, God commissions him to take possession of the land and warns him to keep faith with the Mosaic Covenant (Joshua 1:3): "Be strong and very courageous" by keeping the Book of the Law near. In order words, "meditate on it day and night so that you may be careful to do everything written in it." Meditation was the act of remembering God's command to release God's blessings.

The account of Joshua reminding the Israelites of God's command was ongoing and continuous. He used different channels to communicate with them—in particular, in his farewell speeches.

Joshua's farewell speeches are outlined on chapters 23–24:

Joshua, in his old age and conscious that he is "going the way of all the earth" (Joshua 23:14), gathers the leaders of the Israelites together and reminds them of Yahweh's great works for them and of the need to love Yahweh (Joshua 23:11). The Israelites are told—just as Joshua himself had been told (Joshua 1:7)—that they must comply with "all that is written in the Book of the Law of Moses" (Joshua 23:6), neither "turning aside from it to the right hand or to the left" (i.e., by adding to the law or diminishing from it).

Joshua meets again with all the people at Shechem in chapter 24 and addresses them a second time. He recounts the history of God's formation of the Israelite nation, beginning with "Terah, the father of Abraham and Nahor, [who] lived beyond the Euphrates River and worshiped other gods" (Joshua 24:2). He invited the Israelites to choose between serving the Lord who had delivered them from Egypt or the gods which their ancestors had served on the other side of the Euphrates or the gods of the Amorites in whose land they now lived. The people chose to serve the Lord, a decision which Joshua recorded in the Book of the Law of God. He then erected a memorial stone "under the oak that was by the sanctuary of the Lord" in Shechem (Joshua 24:1–27). The oak is associated with the Oak of Moreh where Abram had set up camp during his travels in this area (Genesis 12:6). Thus "Joshua made a covenant with the people," literally "cut a covenant," a phrase common to the Hebrew, Greek, and Latin languages. It derives from the custom of sacrifice, in which the victims were cut in pieces and offered to the deity invoked in ratification of the engagement.

Emotional Intelligence: Its Impact on Leadership Communication

Highly effective leaders are those that are capable of managing their emotions effectively in various situations and settings. For example, they are "skilled at sharing and responding to emotions; they know how to communicate affection, liking, and excitement to followers and how to channel their feelings to achieve their objectives and to maintain friendly group relations (Hackman and Johnson 2013, 28). In such, leaders are responsible for creating a climate of trust conducive to motivating and developing collaborative efforts. Leaders with high emotional intelligence can create such an atmosphere through their day-to-day interactions and the empowering of others to act. Kouzes and Posner (2012) argue that such leaders "make trust and teamwork high priorities. They posit that trust is required to build collaboration and promote people working cooperatively together and is a strong predictor of employee satisfaction, quality of communication, honest sharing of information, acceptance of change, and team and organizational performance" (pp. 219–220).

Many scholars classify leaders with emotional intelligence abilities as transformational leaders. They are recognized as having an aptitude to tap into their followers and lead transformationally and effectively. Jayakody and Gamage (2015) cite Lowe and Kroeck (1996), who conclude that "transformational leaders are consistently rated by subordinates as being more effective leaders and have always been linked with higher performance and success." Those leaders "believe in the need for change. They then establish a clear vision for the future of the organization and provide a model that is consistent with the vision. They promote the acceptance of group goals and provide individualized support afterward. As a result, followers of transformational leaders often feel trust and respect toward the leader and are motivated to do more than they are expected to do" (Jayakody and Gamage 2015).

Social Intelligence: Its Impact on Leadership Communication

There are several definitions of social intelligence that have surfaced as far back as the 1920s. In particular, Ford and Tisak (1983) define social intelligence in terms of behavioral outcomes: "one's ability to accomplish relevant objectives in specific social settings," which include the awareness of others and their response and adaptation to different situations and contexts (Beheshtifar 2012). The last decade has experienced an explosion of the need for leaders to obtain skills that can transfer globally. Leaders ought to stretch across the globe to support international expansions and cross-cultural communications, such as the need to "understand business, political, and cultural environments worldwide—the need to learn the perspectives, tastes, trends, and technologies of many other cultures—and the need to work simultaneously with people from different cultures" (Northouse 2013). A high level of social intelligence helps leaders to maneuver in a cross-cultural environment, enabling them to be flexible and collaborative in their approaches and help to facilitate and deliver exceptional results in various settings and situations.

Rooted in the Bible is one's ability to bring the "body of Christ" together, which is considered as a "unit, though it is made up of many parts; and though all its parts are many, they form one body. So, it is with Christ. Those parts of the body that seem to be weaker are indispensable" (1 Corinthians 12:12, 22). Leaders' ability to relate to different people to establish a successful relationship is a necessity and is consistent with Paul's teaching that modeled Jesus's ministry of inclusion.

Interpersonal Intelligence: Its Impact on Leadership Communication

Similarly, to emotional intelligence and social intelligence, interpersonal intelligence plays a vital role in helping leaders to attain organizational performance goals. The successful imparting of information requires exceptional interpersonal skills—a set of behaviors consisting of both emotional and physical responses in which people use to communicate. Interpersonal skills are defined by effective communication, exceptional listening aptitude, and expert leadership dexterity (Jonson 2016). Interpersonal skills are necessary for continuous workplace collaboration and performance improvement through ongoing clarification of established expectations and the constant sharing of a compelling vision that aims to generate enthusiasm and support from the team. Frequent interactions involve a leader using interpersonal skills to prevent derision and promote unity within the organization (Walker 2012).

Effective communication is the central theme that is present in emotional, social, interpersonal, and all other skills that characterize leadership competencies. Leading others requires the adherence competent, skillful, and capable communication, which entails the interchange of thoughts, opinions, or information by way of speech, writing, or sign (Johnson 2016).

B. Appreciation for Work

Upon creation, God looked at the work of His hands and said, "It is good." Such a statement implies that work was meant to be enjoyable and "good." It is safe to assume that the biblical perspective of work is designed to be a positive exponential experience, empowered by the Holy Spirit for the well-being of others. Witherington III (2011) defines work as "any necessary and meaningful task that God calls and gifts a person to do and which can be undertaken to the glory of God and for the edification and aid of human being, being inspired by the Spirit and foreshadowing the realities of the new creation."

The first essential element that must be considered is the ability to recognize we are all created by God and are equipped to do "greater things" according to Jesus. The Bible accentuates that fact in the Gospel of John 14: "Very truly I tell you, whoever believes in me will do the works I have been doing, and they will do even greater things than these because I am going to the Father." If we are to discover and practice a biblical, Christian perspective on work and vocation, organizations would be productive. For the power of the Holy Spirit in every worker—causes him/her to be productive and to supernaturally use wisdom and discernment—to make ethical decisions that yield results. Humility/meekness, forgiveness, patience, hope, courage/faith, generosity, sympathy/compassion, love, truthfulness, gentleness, kindness, self-control, and joy are values that must be practiced in the workplace by leaders because they are inherently from God (Fedler 2006). One can only describe God's interpretation of work as working with excellence.

The word excellence is referred to as being the "secret of joy in work." The Lord God assessed the results of the work He had created and referred to it as "good." One of God's creations was "mankind in His image" to "rule over" the rest of His created resources. In other words, the Lord God created humankind to work. Work is one of God's values and is intrinsic to humanity. Witherington III (2011) puts it this way: "all persons in Christ are called to both ministry and discipleship of various sorts."

"Labor is part of this calling, some of which will be remunerative, some of which will not be. If we see work as part of our life stewardship, just as play and worship and prayer and sleep and so many other things are part of our stewardship, we will begin to be on track" (p. 81).

Work is meant to be part of our joy of salvation when it's done in a culture of excellence. One that is created not as an "act but as a habit," which Schein (1990) explains as "a pattern of underlying assumptions…invented, discovered, or developed by a given group that holds common assumptions that result in automatic patterns of perceiving, thinking, feeling, and behaving provide meaning stability and comfort." Appreciation for work is only possible in a culture of excellence, one that celebrates and espouses garden values. Mintrom and Cheng (2014) define the culture of excellence as "an organizational context encouraging behaviors that, when deployed, continuously improve task performance." Biblically speaking, the Bible's account of creation is an example of flawless execution, one that humankind was tasked to rule over, according to Genesis 1:28. Humankind was created with godly attributes and was commanded to be fruitful and multiply while adhering to those values that creation was built upon. John 15 tells us that humankind's ability to be fruitful and to multiply is contingent upon his ability to remain connected to those values: "remain in me, as I also remain in you. No branch can bear fruit by itself; it must remain in the vine. Neither can you bear fruit unless you remain in me. If you remain in me and I in you, you will bear much fruit; apart from me, you can do nothing. If you do not remain in me, you are like a branch that is thrown away and withers; such branches are picked up, and thrown into the fire and burned. If you remain in me and my words remain in you, ask whatever you wish, and it will be done for you."

The need to stay connected is a command—one, if not uphold, could have dire consequences. Unconnected through disobedience, Adam and Eve were "banished from the garden of Eden" and suffered the consequences of their behaviors. One of the ways to sustain garden values that produces "fruit and multiplication" is to create shared cultures.

Creating a shared culture begins with a clear quality message and direction in which a leader communicates a clear vision. Following the creation of man, the Lord God articulated a clear vision to Adam that included the account of Genesis 2:

1. *Teamwork and alignment as necessary to bear fruit and produce good work.* The Lord God said, "It is not good for man to be alone. I will make a helper suitable for him."
2. *Empowerment.* "Now the Lord God had formed out of the ground all the wild animals and all the birds in the sky. He brought them to the man to see what he would them; and whatever the man called each living creature, that was its name."
3. *Work and uphold garden values.* "The Lord God took the man and put him in the Garden of Eden to work it and take care of it. And the Lord God commanded the man, 'You are free to eat from any tree in the garden; but you must not eat from the tree of the knowledge of good and evil, for when you eat from it, you will certainly die.'"

God's direction to Adam was well-structured with a clearly stated message that included what to do and the consequences for his actions. As part of communicating with a team, leaders must be accessible to provide the necessary information and to model proper behaviors. The goal is to ensure that information is shared to build trust in the leadership; dialogue encouraged to eliminate silos, promote agility, flexibility, and fluidity.

C. A Global Impact

Globalization is not a new concept. It is "a word which describes an old process of the interrelatedness of people and business throughout the world that ultimately infuses into global cultural, political, and economic realms" (Ellwood 2010). Globalization was evident from the beginning of time and was premeditated by God upon creation. His mandate to Adam and Eve was to "be fruitful and increase in number; fill the earth and subdue it. Rule over the fish of the sea and the birds of the air and over every living creature that moves on the ground; I give you every seed-bearing plant on the face of the whole earth and every tree that has fruit with seed in it. They will be yours for food. And for all the beasts of the earth and all the birds of the air and all the creatures that move on the ground—everything that has the breath of life in it—I give every green plant for food" (Genesis 1:28–30). To realize the mandate, God created "man" in His image with similar characters and attributes. One of which is the ability to think globally with a "global mindset," "fill the entire earth and subdue it." A global mindset is the collection of individual characteristics and attributes—cognitive, personality, and social traits—that enable global leaders to influence groups, individuals, and organizations from other parts of the world.

Moreover, God's mandate to Noah to "be fruitful and increase in number and fill the earth" reinforce His desires for leaders to make a global impact and not to be confined in one area with one kind of people but instead to reach outside of their comfort zone to change and transform others, as exemplified in the story of Babel (Genesis 11). Cabrera and Unruh (2012) assert, "global trade has been around, and after all, since the sixteenth century (and broad cross-border trade for thousands of years before that). One of the most compelling evidence is how today's national energy policy decision by a remote country without significant petroleum reserves affects discussions taking place tens of thousands of miles away, posit Cabrera and Unruh (2012).

It can be said that leadership (as God wished for) is "always part of a larger community context, and for multicultural teams, members bring varied context assumptions to both leading and following" (Lingenfelter 2008, 9). The account of Genesis 1:28 "be fruitful and increase in number..." correlates with the concept of leading cross-culturally—which allows leaders to build communities of trust, resulting in the empowerment to becoming fruitful in the pursuit of a vision.

Globalization Defined

Karadagli (2012) posits globalization is the integration of trade, finance, social-cultural, and technological processes that connect people across continents. For instance, the global exchange of goods and services has increased from 30 percent of the world's gross domestic product (GDP) to 60 percent during the past forty years with foreign direct investment in companies across borders totaled $22 trillion for the period ending in 2012 (Van Paasschen 2015). Additionally, Suci, Asmara, and Mulatsih (2015) define globalization as the process of merging the economies of different countries and their cultures to provide needed goods and services. Other scholars, like Ghaffari and Naderi (2013), steer the definition in another direction, posit that globalization is best defined as the exchange of political, cultural, and economic ideas which occur between international organizations. Cristian and Raluca (2012) suggest that globalization can be described as the absence of barriers and borders of trade. It is not so much the removal or surmounting of geographic borders as it is the insignificance and lack of importance ascribed to them (p. 589).

The Great Commission is a simple, unpretentious message of obedience. "Go and preach the Good News to all nation/creation." Mark 16:16 is a comparable command that came following Jesus's death for mankind. It is safe to assume that both, the New and the Old Testament, fundamental elements of leadership capture a globalized and inclusive vision of God's intention for leadership approach.

One that is rooted in profound obedience to the inerrancy of His Word, which Jesus came to fulfill. He affirms in the Gospel of Matthew 5:17, "Do not think that I have come to abolish the Law or the Prophets; I have not come to abolish them but to fulfill them." In fulfilling the law, Jesus exemplified the characteristics of global leaders. As man and God, one can define Him as being culture agile. He was able to perform successfully in diverse and cross-cultural situations. Regardless of His audience, Jesus remained faithful to the kingdom's message; nevertheless, He adjusted His verbiage accordingly to meet the need of His audience. As a result, He attracted many from different walks of life to follow Him.

Global leadership is defined as the interactions which occur between different people and cultures regardless of the leadership style used to influence the desired outcome (Adler as cited in Mendenhall 2013). Additionally, Minner (2015) describes global leadership as the process of influencing the behaviors and attitudes of a global community to achieve common objectives. Global leaders possess the ability to make a positive impact on their organizations and in people's lives. They think globally and can be strengthened and equipped individuals to replicate their achievements. It also requires having a global mindset with the ability to perceive, analyze, and decode behaviors and situations in multiple cultural contexts, help leaders to experience success in a global setting (Cabrera and Unruh 2012, 36). Individuals with a global mindset can work with and influence people, organizations, and institutions that are different from their own. They are sensitive to differences, they understand how culture shapes behavior, and they are able to suspend premature judgment, build bridges across cultural boundaries, and nurture trust with others. They are not proficient in all cultures, but they find ways to transcend culture to build productive relationships.

To have what it takes to successfully lead in a global environment requires more than just theory. It requires that leaders proactively reach out to groups different from their own to understand the deeper aspects of the cultures they seek to enter for culture consists of different layers—above and below the surface. Our ability to "accurately read the cross-cultural or multicultural situation; assess the differences in behaviors attitudes, and values, and to respond successfully within the cross-cultural context differentiate successful and less successful global leaders" (Caliguri 2012, 5).

D. Ethics and Power

Ethics and power form the necessary foundation of leader-follower relationships. They are interdependent and ethical behavior is often seen as associated with differential access to power (Ciulla 2004). Sensibly, ethical dealing is what helps to create a culture of trust among leaders and their followers, resulting in "power-sharing through good teamwork."

It is not enough to bring a group of highly skilled people together to create a team. It is essential that the team work well together and trust one another to be successful and to achieve its purpose. A culture of trust exists when the team is sure about the leader's actions, now and in the future—consequently reducing ambiguity and uncertainty (Saskin and Sashkin 2003). Hakanen et al. (2015) believe communication and trust are essential for the building of high-performing teams. They also believe that trust is the foundation that enables people to work together, and it is an enabler for social interactions that can be seen as a driver of performance and business results. Additionally, Hakanen and Soudunsaari (2012) define the critical areas for trust-building as "personal knowledge, regular face-to-face interaction, empathy, respect, and genuine listening."

E. Ethical Behavior/Culture

The world over will be a better place when businesses across the world embrace and behave in ways that model the values God's fashioned. Instilling and creating a culture that espouses ethical behavior requires commitment. It's not just enough to lead, but also, to lead with values and beliefs that are communicated and shared among the team for culture derives from the ideas, values of the leader. Therefore, a culture that promotes ethical behavior and shared power can only be achievable when leaders "externalize their assumptions and embed them gradually and consistently into the mission, goals, structures, and decision processes of the organization" (NEO and CHEN 2007). For example, Jesus spent approximately four years training His future leaders—instilling one vision—God's kingdom. He walked the talk by his behaviors, decisions He made, and how He shared power by assigning them tasks. He modeled the way and inspired a shared vision during His time with them.

Ethics is one of those subjects that is very complex and hard to reach harmony. Waggoner (2010) suggests four words that he believes connects to the term ethics and that are used interchangeably: ethics, virtues, morals, values, and principles. Each term builds on another to advance good ethics, which serves as a basis for all human relations. Thus, the relationship between leaders and followers, remarks Ciulla (2004).

Biblical Ethics

Ethics matters to God's kingdom as much as earthly organizations. From creation, God set the stage and followed a work pattern that He intended humankind to follow. He expressed liking in the work He performed and consequent accomplishments. Genesis 1 notes that "God saw all that He had made, and it was very good."

The term ethics in the Bible is associated with integrity, obedience to God's laws, and being upright and blameless. It means to follow established rules regardless of who benefits from the outcome. Proverbs 10:9 apprises, "Whoever walks in integrity walks securely, but he who makes his ways crooked will be found out."

God boasts about leaders who walk in integrity. He guides them to success and blesses the fruit of their hands. Job is described as such a "man" by God Himself. In Job 1, He refers to Job as a man who "feared God and shunned from evil." He lived a life that can be described as proactive obedience. He would make arrangements for his sons to be purified in case they had disobeyed God while holding parties with their friends. Job would sacrifice a burnt offering for each of them, thinking perhaps my children have sinned and cursed God in their hearts (Job 1:4–5).

Definition of Ethics

Similarly, to leadership, ethics has been defined by many scholars and continue to evolve with time and globalization. Ethics means different things to different people, various organizations and cultures, different social status, beliefs, racial identification, and so forth. What may be appropriate in one culture may not be accepted in another. Bishop cites the definitions and theories about what constitutes ethics abound. Different people have different interpretations of the term—to the superficial meaning of "right and wrong" to an older term, such as "doing the right thing even when people are not watching."

Ciulla (2004) notes that ethics is a "reflective process," as well as a "communal exercise," in which we attempt to "work out the rights and obligations we have and share with others." Additionally, "Ethics, then, tries to find a way to protect one person's rights and needs against and alongside the rights and needs of others."

Roles of Leadership in Creating an Ethical Culture

An ethical culture means that it is led by leaders who put culture first and not profit. Bishop (2013) explains that part of what went wrong with Enron: the ethical dilemma they faced was caused by the leaders who put the bottom line ahead of ethical behavior and doing what was right. There is a need for organizations to understand that culture should not be overlooked because the consequences are too costly to ignore. Johnson & Johnson understands such concept and creates what the company refers to as it's Credo. The *credo* is a way to showcase its founder's intent "to alleviate pain and disease—expended the idea into a business ideology that placed service to customers and concern for employees ahead of returns to shareholders," explains Collings and Porras. Johnson & Johnson's ethical expectations (Credo) entail what the company refers to as the "Four Tenets: customers, employees, community, stockholders."

Johnson & Johnson's leadership commitment to the Credo is an example of leading a culture of ethical accountability. When companies commit to ensuring ethical behaviors, equitability, fairness, and integrity, the focus is always on human aspects instead of financials. Real sustainability stems from human value, according to Talwar (2009). Across the globe, he insists, there is a dire need to improve the material and spiritual conditions of humanity. Focusing on matters that concern human value, such as culture, helping individual employees and other stakeholders to unleash their capabilities and unearth the latent potential of the organization. It eliminates many troubles and social problems and leads to an ethical way of governance in the organization's culture, policies, systems, and actions, which ultimately will lead to the total transformation of the corporate world and provide prosperity and better quality of life for society at large.

Moreover, creating a culture of ethics means reaching the "hearts" of followers for "ethics lie at the heart of all human relationships and hence at the heart of the relationship between leaders and followers," utters Ciulla. Leaders must demonstrate excellence in leading—which means holding themselves accountable to practice what they preached—driving with purpose, principles, and passion through others. Leadership ethical accountability is a driver for companies' ethical behaviors and productive organizational culture, infers Thompson (2013). The seventeenth chairman of the Joint Chiefs of Staff, Navy Admiral Mike Mullen, stated, "Leadership is about understanding accountability, being held accountable, and at the same time holding yourself accountable."

The Fruit of Ethical Behaviors

All leaders are created in God's image with the same power and authority to do greater things than what Jesus was able to accomplish during His time on earth. John 14:12 validates, "Very truly I tell you, whoever believes in me will do the works I have been doing, and they will do even greater things than these because I am going to the Father." Therefore, leaders must follow His directives in the course of leading followers to fulfill their organizational visions.

Ethical fruit for leaders must be one of the indispensable components of their behaviors and virtues. Fedler (2006) identifies these behaviors—as virtues as humility/meekness, forgiveness, patience, hope, courage/faith, generosity, sympathy/compassion, love, truthfulness, gentleness, kindness, self-control, and joy—as Christian leader's imperative because they are inherently from God.

Ethical behaviors in organizational cultures translate to leading with integrity, help to build trust among members of the team, and create an atmosphere of trust amid leaders and the people they are called to lead. Trust has a positive influence on the culture and is essential to effective communication, culture assimilation, and cooperation. Employees follow leaders they can trust to do the right thing. I believe that trust opens the way for open and honest interactions between leaders and followers, in particular, where other barriers are present, such as cultural differences, diverse languages, sexual orientation, and religious beliefs.

Leaders are more likely to be fruitful in an environment where there is trust because followers tend to be amenable to integrate.

The Bible uses the word *trust* interchangeably with *faith*. Faith is one of the critical attributes to living a successful and obedient Christian life. Hebrews 11 affirms, "Without faith, it is impossible to please God because anyone who comes to him must believe that He exists and that He rewards those who earnestly seek him." To espouse trust, leaders ought to "walk the walk" and "talk the talk." Kouzes and Posner (2003) posit that earning trust requires leaders to be accessible to their constituents, actions such as listening and talking to people, having a consistent physical presence in the workplace, and allowing people to get to know them.

How Can Organizations Enforce Ethical Behaviors?

As Christians, we have the power of the Holy Spirit to help us to do the right thing as a matter of the "heart" and not out of obligation. We "cannot do it on our own," Paul affirms. Fedler (2006) cited the apostle in Romans 7:24, "Wretched man that I am! Who will rescue me from this body of death? Only God can do it through the death and resurrection of Jesus Christ." The apostle Paul believes that "we are a new creation" by the power of Jesus's resurrection. He was all about the kingdom and not personal gain. He experienced success throughout his ministry; he rejoiced at the end of his life as he looked back on his accomplishment: "I have fought the good fight, I have finished the race, I have kept the faith. Now there is in store for me the crown of righteousness, which the Lord, the righteous Judge, will award to me on that day" (2 Timothy 4:7–8).

Additionally, there is a need for organizations to emphasize ethical behaviors at the executive level and across organizations. Holding on to strong ethical standards, and rewards people accordingly while holding them accountable when required. There should not be any compromise ethical principles for the sake of achieving success. However, leaders ought to focus less on the bottom line and extend full recognition for teamwork and honest feedback.

F. Power and Leadership

In many developing countries, the concept of leadership is often linked with power. These leaders use power to oppress their people and often misrepresent and ignore their voices, the common good, peace, and stability of the country and have equally hindered most people from economic growth and opportunities (Ejimabo 2013). Corruptions and partiality is a way of life. Ejimabo (2013) also noted "some leaders, lawmakers, and policymakers with money and power do not appear to have the interest of the common people at heart. Laws are made for the common people and not for the leaders. The decision-making process under the current situation was not based on the analysis of the needs of the people. Instead, it is based on political advantage and exists to favor the rich and the special interests of those in authority in the entire country." Power is defined as the ability to get things done the way one wants them to be done (Dahl 1957).

Often, the misuse of power in leadership results in a lack of ethical behavior, transparency, and accountability in governance. The difference between proper and improper use of power is the difference between success and failure, high and low productivity, motivation, and disillusion (Singh 2009). Such misappropriation and quest for power are as old as creation itself. It was the devious serpent that influenced Eve, who persuaded Adam to partake of the forbidden fruit (Singh 2009). Adam and Eve were easily misled to disobey God's command as a result of they thought could be the benefit of having the same power as God and overlooking all other factors that were made available to them. Although the need for structure and power is needed to run the most trivial functions of an organization or project, it could be both, a prerequisite for success, but is equally effective in destroying the organization as well just as in the case of Adam and Eve. Their quests for power and consequent insubordination led humanity in rebellion and rejection of God's laws.

The negative effect of power is ostensible throughout God's choices for leaders. To remain in power, King Saul sought to kill David in the account of 1 Samuel 19–24: "Saul told his son Jonathan and all the attendants to kill David. But Jonathan had taken a great liking to David and warned him, 'My father Saul is looking for a chance to kill you. Be on your guard tomorrow morning; go into hiding and stay there. I will go out and stand with my father in the field where you are. I'll speak to him about you and will tell you what I find out.'" Power also drove Absalom to plot to kill his father, David: "After this, Absalom got a chariot and horses for himself and fifty men to run before him. Absalom would get up early and stand near the city gate. Anyone who had a problem for the king to settle would come here. When someone came, Absalom would call out and say, 'what city are you from?' Then Absalom would say, 'I'm from one of the tribes of Israel.' Then Absalom would say, 'look, your claims are right, but the king has no one to listen to you. I wish someone would make me judge in this land! Then the people with problems could come to me, and I could help them get justice'" (2 Samuel 15–19).

Powers, when misused or when negative, has the potential to lessen the quality of a culture or an organization. Negative power, by definition, curbs creativity, stalls personality growth, limits ethical practice, prevents career advancement, manipulates the psyche, bears false witness, overtly or covertly exhibits bias, and acts arbitrarily and capriciously from a position of power (Singh 2009).

G. Love

Despite fading from a socio-political to a post-modern and disengaged message, love permeates contemporary society as one of the most celebrated human feelings and experiences, explains Tasselli (2018). He argues that love is central to people's everyday lives and business experiences. One of the most famous biblical passages is Matthew 22:37. The passage of Matthew 22 highlights Jesus's response to the Pharisees, whose mission was to snare Him to justify their pursuits to put Him to death. It states, "Love the Lord your God with all your heart and with all your soul and with all your mind. This is the first and greatest commandment. And the second is like it: Love your neighbor as yourself. All the Law and the Prophets hang on these two commandments." Jesus used the passage to deflect the lawmakers and to highlight the significance of leading with love and compassion.

Love is habitually implied to be a "powerful emotion involving an intense attachment to an object and a high evaluation of it. Love does not involve emotion at all but is only an active interest in the well-being of the object. It essentially a relationship involving mutuality and reciprocity, rather than emotion" (Craig 2000). The Bible references four unique forms of love that are communicated through four Greek words: Eros, Storge, Philia, and Agape. For this purpose, I will highlight Philia's love, which is the type of "intimate love in the Bible that most Christians practice toward each other. This Greek term describes the powerful emotional bond seen in deep friendships. Philia love is the most general type of love in Scripture, encompassing love for fellow humans, care, respect, and compassion for people in need. The concept of brotherly love that unites believers is unique to Christianity" (Zavada 2019). Philia "is a relevant construct for organizational life: it looks at interpersonal relationships as embedded in larger structures of trust involving the overall community. It is a powerful source of organizational functioning (Tasselli 2018).

Jesus said, in John 13:34–35, "A new command I give you: Love one another. As I loved you, so you must love one another. By this everyone will know that you are my disciples if you love one another." This statement demonstrates the need for leaders to "love" first and lead. Leading without love is prone to failure for love empowers leaders to go beyond the natural causes "everything to bind together in perfect harmony" (Colossians 3:14). Transformational leaders understand the concept of leading in harmony. According to Bass (1985), transformational leadership is exclusively about the leaders and their behaviors. He suggests that transformational leaders adjust their style to various situations based on the task and the followers. Love is what governs faith. According to Graves and Addington (2002), "The worlds of leadership and faith were meant to be married. Never separated, never odds, and never in competition. They were never intended to stand on opposite sides of the room—they are together for appropriate and practical application" (xi). Faith is the foundations of ethical leadership—the types that produce extraordinary results and cultivates a culture of trust where the leader is seen as someone who can be trusted, who has integrity, and is honest and truthful.

The result of leading with love is limitless. As outlined in 1 Corinthians 13:8, "Love never fails. It remains patient, kind, does not envy, it does not boast, it is not self-seeking, it is not easily angered, it keeps no record of wrongs, it protects, always trusts, always hopes, always persevere" (vv. 4–8).

Leading with a focus on Philia love:

1.) Helps organizations to create agile cultures for holistic approaches. For "the capacities of an organization reside in more than the quality of the leadership and the observable structures and processes; they are also embedded in the beliefs of the organization, its attitude towards learning and approach to fostering continuous change" (NEO and CHEN 2007). Change is inevitable and has the propensity to impede with status quo approaches that keep an organization from reaching its full potential. Therefore, managing changes stem from our globalized universe requires leaders to focus on not just the bottom line, but the vehicles that harvest culture agility.

2.) It creates an opportunity for leaders to serve. Christ came to help. "He epitomized the concept of leadership by His statement: "The Son of man did not come to be served but to serve, and to give his life as a ransom for many" (Mark 10:45) (Engstrom 1976).

Engstrom also posits, "His kind of service set an example. He was willing to wash his disciples' feet. His perfect, sinless human life ended in self-sacrifice at Calvary. He showed His followers how to serve, and He demanded no less of those who would carry on His work on earth. Jesus teaches all leaders for all time that greatness is not found in rank or position but service. He makes it clear that real leadership is grounded in love, which must issue in service" (p. 37). He is known to be a servant leader—which is about both "serving" and "leading"—while its origin can be traced back to Robert K. Greenleaf and his 1970 article "The Servant as a Leader" (Ragnarsson et al. 2018). For Greenleaf, "The Servant leader is Servant first...It begins with the natural feeling that one wants to serve" (Duby 2009 cites Greenleaf 1977). In servant leadership, leading others is about providing leadership and service to followers simultaneously and helping them to accomplish their tasks, visions, and goals (Ragnarsson et al. cite Buchen 1998; Farling Stone and Winston 1999; Greenleaf 2008; Kahl 2004).

Additionally, Northouse (2013) defines servant leadership as an approach focusing on leadership behaviors that leaders are attentive to the concerns of their followers, empathize with them, and nurture them. He mentions servant leaders put followers first, empower them, and help them develop their full personal capacities. Likewise, Sipe and Frick (2015) believe that servant leaders practice acceptance and empathy, as well as showing tolerance of other's imperfections. They are inclusive in their approach and use power as a means to serve as the leaders put the good of those led over self-interest (van Dierendonck and Patterson 2015).

Kouzes and Posner (2017) posits that love is ultimately the secret of leadership. They explain that great leaders demonstrate to others that they genuinely care about other's welfare by their actions rather than merely by their words. They argue and emphasize that leadership has a powerful effect on people's lives when others believe that their leader personally cares about them. According to Anderson et al. (2019), "Love unlocks the good, the true, and the beautiful by seeing it in others." They emphasize that love is recognized as a universal virtue encompassing many types of relationships and varying depths of commitment. Leaders who extend love to their followers cause them to feel more connected and, consequently, increase organizational performance.

Chapter 3
The Garden Culture: An Inclusive Approach to Leadership Practice

Creating and maintaining a thriving and shared culture is one of the critical duties of a global leader for leaders play a crucial role in determining whether the culture of an organization, as experienced by employees, contributes to or undermines employees well-being (Davenport 2015). Schein (2010) speaks of culture as an "abstraction." He defines culture as "a pattern of shared underlying assumptions that a group has learned as it solves problems of external pressure and internal cooperation. These assumptions have worked well enough to be considered valid and so have evolved into norms and principles for behavior. He notes that culture is dominated by our beliefs, our day-to-day interactions, rules placed by our family, nation, and ethnic group. He also believes that culture is not an easy concept to decipher because its creation is connected to one's experience and continues to evolve with new elements as we encounter new people and acquire new experiences.

Tsai (2011) refers to culture as "socially learned and transmitted by members that provide the rules for behavior within organizations." He believes that culture plays a vital role in an organization, a function that determines whether the environment is conducive and healthy in which to work. He argues "when the interaction between the leadership and employees is good, the latter will make a greater contribution to team communication and collaboration, and will also be encouraged to accomplish the mission and objectives assigned by the organization, thereby enhancing job satisfaction."

God created man and gave him the mission of being the keeper of the newly formed culture. The garden culture is one that has its foundation on "love" and "obedience/faith" as sustained by the passages of John 3:16: "For God so loved the world that He gave His Only Son" and on John 3:18 that concludes, "Whoever believes in Him is not condemned."

Because culture is a "learned belief," God worked hand in hand with Adam to institute guidelines—which can be described as humankind's handbook for creating a culture of excellence. Also, God establishes levers/guidelines to enable the work Adam was tasked to implement: "Then God said, I give you every seed-bearing plant on the face of the whole earth and every tree that has fruit with seed in it. They will be yours for food. And to all the beasts of the earth and all the birds in the sky and all the creatures that move along the ground—everything that has the breath of life in it—I give every green plant for food" (Genesis 1:29–30). This mandate created an opportunity for Adam and Eve (leaders) to develop dynamic governance that aims to create a gradual and consistent approach as modeled by God during the first six days of creation. Productivity, appreciation for work, culture of excellence were part of God's results. In other words, God created a culture with high fulfillment outcome to be led by Adam, whom He created in His image and likeness.

A thriving and shared culture is one in which values are espoused; all members follow the rules; norms, symbols, and traditions are recognizable among people (Northouse 2013). The concept of culture is so essential that God created the conditions, communicated the rules, and established different levers to help Adam and Eve to develop dynamic governance to realize the mandate of Genesis 1:29–30.

There are two main levers for developing dynamic governance capabilities: (1) able people and (2) agile processes (NEO and CHEN 2007). "Dynamic governance" is defined as "deliberate leadership intention and ambition to structure social and economic interactions to achieve desired goals...it reflects the leader's conscious efforts to shape their future—to try to structure human interaction—the alternate is anarchy and chaos" (p. 10). This definition is in alignment with the culture that God created. The Bible explains that in six days, God created all resources necessary for mankind to live a fulfilling life, and to "be fruitful." In six days, the Lord God formed a culture supported by different "levers" intended to uphold the sustainability of the created culture, which He intended and gave to man to maintain entirely.

Definition of Lever

The *Collins English Dictionary* defines a lever "as a handle or bar that is attached to a piece of machinery and which you push or pull to operate the machine." This handle/bar is used to help move heavy or firmly fixed load with one end when pressure is applied to the other (*Oxford Dictionary*). Levers are like gears that can be used to increase the force available from a mechanical power source. They are described as a "rigid piece that transmits and modifies force or motion" (*Merriam Webster*).

Culture

At the heart of every organization are the people who make up the culture, which can be used to refer to the interpersonal, team, and organizational levels (Hultman 2002). Success is unlikely without culture alignment. Where there is misalignment, mutual misunderstandings become the norm, and organizational performance suffers as a result if prompt steps are not taken to overcome them. As the author of the "Garden Culture," God understood the need to sustain the (created) culture with levers (principles) that were strong enough to withstand the demand of His mandate. His rules that required obedience and trust and collaboration: "The Lord God took the man and put him in the Garden of Eden to work it and take care of it. And the Lord God commanded the man, you are free to eat from any tree [lever] in the garden, but you must not eat [lever] from the tree of the knowledge of good and evil, for when you eat from it, you will certainly die [lever]."

He established and communicated the culture from the beginning. By doing so, He accentuated on the fact that culture is the "foundation of the social order that we live in and of the rules we abide by and that it was the responsibility of the leader to ensure successful integration between people and culture through various forms of learning" (Schein 2010). Schein also argues that culture can be analyzed using several different levels ranging from tangible, overt manifestations that you can see and feel, to the deeply embedded, unconscious, underlying assumptions.

A shared culture is one where people with diverse backgrounds, points of view, and experiences work together to support and rally behind the vision of an organization. The organization's vision is articulated, lived, and translated into shared-action plans with a team that produces outstanding results with a high level of people satisfaction, a clear sense of purpose.

On the sixth day, God created heaven and earth as well as people (His ultimate creation). God loves humankind, and His love is expressed tangibly throughout the Bible. First John 3:1 says, "See what great love the Father has lavished on us, that we should be called children of God." And that is what we are.

CHAPTER 4
Characteristics of Successful Global Leaders

One of the most persuasive pieces of evidence of globalization today is the interdependency of global economies, further illustrating the unique point we are in historically. House, Javidan, and Dorfman (2001) write, "With the ongoing globalization of the world's marketplace, there has been a shift from supplying overseas markets from a domestic base to establishing subsidiaries in numerous countries, acquiring or merging with foreign firms, or establishing international joint ventures."

A study by KPMG indicates that 41 percent of all mergers and acquisitions in 2000 were cross-border, and this compared to 24 percent in 1996 (Javidan, Stahl, Brodbeck and Wilderom 2005). While the fall of 2008 substantiated the challenges of interdependent markets, the beneficial effects of globalization are also astounding, providing opportunities that leaders around the world dare not to ignore. Members around the world "have more frequent contact and exposure to one another through the internet, satellite hookups, and fiber optic lines. Increased international travel with millions of people visiting other nations each year; multinational organizations and open markets; and rapidly expanding broadcasting bandwidth," to name a few (Hackman and Johnson 2013).

Leaders are called to "make things happen" through people. For at the heart of leadership is one's ability to manage differences and comportments taping into inherent core attributes that man possesses from creation to lead globally. The core attributes associated with the global mindset outlined in the previous chapter are (1) psychological capital, (2) intellectual capital, and (3) social capital.

Psychological capital. Psychological capital is focused mostly around our openness to diversity, respect for others and their cultures, willingness to work with people across culture, self-efficacy, cognitive flexibility, and cultural agility.

Intellectual capital. Intellectual capital consists of our knowledge and understanding of the world around us in which we transact business. In the context of globalization, intellectual capital enables us to learn and understand the multiplicity of environmental elements—politics, regional makeup, tribal groups dynamic, business competitors, rules of engagement around culture, business policies and relations, business industry specific knowledge, to name a few that could be a potential friend or foe in our business arena.

Social capital. Global social capital is the set of resources that accrue to global leaders by their social connections. The construct enables global leaders, through their connections, network to access and share a range of relevant information (ranging from trends, threats, opportunities, to name a few) in the global marketplace. The ability to form genuine, trusting, and quality social connections—a relationship is a sine qua non to a global leader's survival.

I appreciate Hackman's and Johnson's definition of leadership as "human communication that modifies the attitudes and behaviors of others to meet shared group goals" (p. 11). Additionally, Oslan, Li, Wang (2014) describe the term as a "process of influencing others from multiple cultures to adapt a shared-vision through structures, methods that facilitate positive change while fostering individual and collective growth." People are the premise of both descriptions and have been since the beginning of time.

The story of creation underscores the value of people in a very tangible fashion. (1) God created mankind in His image as documented in Genesis 1:26–28: "Then God said, 'Let us make mankind in our image, in our likeness, and let them rule over the fish of the sea and the birds of the sky and over the cattle and over all the earth.'" (2) In His original design, God placed man in a garden that contained all necessary resources and commanded man to "rule over" all. God heightened the value of people from the beginning. He is interested in the comfort of His people—such is evident through biblical stories. Jesus came to fulfill God's promise in Genesis 3:15 and decreed, "I will put enmity between you and the woman, and between your offspring and hers; he will crush your head, and you will strike his heel." Lindsley (2012) argues that "our worth is connected to our Creator. If God is of great and inestimable worth, then human beings made in his image must be of great value, too."

Global leadership characteristics help to equip leaders in becoming successful in their attempts to spreading the Gospel. Those attributes are essential to reach "all people" and to "go into all the world, and make disciples of all nations." The success of global leaders is contingent upon their abilities to recognize and understand different intricacies of culture, i.e., norms and assumptions, which Schein (2010) refers to as culture intelligence. He defines culture intelligence as the development of understanding, empathy, and ability to work with others from other cultures. Culture intelligence requires "four capacities: (1) actual knowledge of some of the essentials of the other cultures involved, (2) cultural sensitivity or mindfulness about culture, (3) motivation to learn about other cultures, and (4) behavioral skills and flexibility to learn new ways of doing things."

Role of Culture

Culture is defined as a "pattern of shared underlying assumptions that a group learned as it solved its problems of external adaptation and integration. Such that work well enough to be considered valid and, therefore, to be taught to new members as the correct way to perceive, think, and feel about these problems" (Schein 2010). Jesus came solely to redeem humanity from the current state (sinful nature) to establish a way of salvation. To do so successfully, He made known and applied the kingdom values in all His actions/decisions. He was all about His Father's business (Luke 2:49).

Why is understanding culture so crucial in the success of global leaders? First and foremost, successful spreading of the Gospel elicits a change in people's behavior—moving from the current state to becoming a "new creation"—the old has passed away, the new has come (2 Corinthians 5:17). First and most, it requires that leaders embrace the need for global characteristics and attributes. In other words, the three core attributes that facilitate a global mindset (psychological, intellectual, and social capital), without which a global mindset is unachievable (see appendix E, "How to Acquire the Core Attributes").

For this reason, the apostle Paul was very successful in spreading the Gospel during his missionary career. He recognized the need to understand the cultural foundations of values, beliefs, and mental models that exist among different people. He declares in 1 Corinthians 9:19–23, "Though I am free and below to no one, I have made myself a slave to everyone, to win as many as possible. To the Jews, I became like a Jew to win the Jews. To those under the law, I became like one under the law, to win those under the law. To those not having the law, I became like one not having the law to win those not having the law. To the weak, I became all weak to win the weak. I have become all things to all people so that by all possible means I might save some. I do all this for the sake of the Gospel that I may share in its blessings."

Paul's success was sustained by many of the characteristics that make global leaders successful. In his case, he learned and put to actions those kingdom values, which he retained from the Savior, whom he encountered on his way to Damascus (Acts 3:4). Paul also defended his abilities and qualifications in Galatians 1:11, stating, "Now I want you to know, brothers, that the Gospel preached by me is not of human origin. I did not receive it from a human being, nor was I taught it, but it came through a revelation of Jesus Christ."

Successful global leaders can understand and discern the different levels of culture summarized by Schein (2010):

1. Artifacts
   a) visible and feelable structures and processes
   b) observed behavior
   c) difficult to decipher

2. Espoused beliefs and values
   a) ideals, goals, values, aspirations
   b) ideologies
   c) rationalizations

3. Basic underlying assumptions
   a) unconscious, taken-for-granted beliefs and values
   b) determined behavior, perception, thought, and feeling

Global leaders also have what it takes to understand and represent all people. According to Caligiuri (2012), today's most significant business opportunities, and also the greatest challenges we face, are global and therefore demand leaders who are also global. Besides, being global means having to build trust, which is an essential aspect of successful leadership. Kouzes and Posner (2003) contend, "We trust people we know." Therefore, gaining consensus in diverse settings requires trust between leaders and constituents, which is vital to building and fostering relationships. The apostle Paul possessed the cultural intelligence that caused him to thrive in complexity while leveraging its fundamental forces to successfully carried out the Great Commission (Cabrera and Unruh 2012, 16). One of the characteristics of being global is having a global mindset, with the ability to perceive, analyze, and decode behaviors and situations in multiple cultural contexts. Having a global mindset helps leaders to experience success in a global setting (Cabrera and Unruh 2012, 36). Individuals with a global mindset can work with and influence people, organizations, and institutions that are different from their own. They are sensitive to differences; they understand how culture shapes behavior and can suspend premature judgment to build bridges across cultural boundaries and nurture trust with others. Those leaders are not proficient in all cultures, but they find ways to transcend culture to build productive relationships.

Secondly, being global obliges that leaders proactively reach out to groups different from their own to understand the deeper aspects of the cultures they seek to enter for culture consists of different layers—above and below the surface. Our ability to "accurately read the cross-cultural or multicultural situation, assess the differences in behaviors, attitudes, and values, and to respond successfully within the cross-cultural context differentiates successful and less successful global leaders" (Caliguri 2012, 5).

Moreover, there is a great need for global leaders to be flexible in their approaches. A resilient leader (as Paul) is one whose focus is on the vision rather than self. One who "inspires a shared vision and who keeps an eye on the horizon rather than outcome, to practice a leadership that inspires a shared vision is like…fishing with a net or being a shepherd of a flock; it is about gathering people together and enlisting them in a movement toward a shared vision" (Kouzes and Posner 2004, 80). The apostle Paul also exemplified such characteristics and was able to realize his mission successfully as a result. In 2 Timothy 4:7–8, he noted, "I have fought a good fight, I have finished my course, I have kept the faith. Now there is in store for me the crown of righteousness, which the Lord, the righteous Judge, will award to me on that day—and not only to me but also to all who have longed for his appearing."

We have been empowered with the ability to accomplish exceedingly more than Jesus was able to achieve during His short time on earth. Global leaders represent a mirror image of Jesus and His attributes. Likewise, to Cabrera's and Unruh's (2012) assumptions, acquiring global competence is a "journey—a moving target." One is not born with global capability but made. One can only be effective through the power of the Holy Spirit and the Word of God. Jesus told the disciples in Luke 24:49 (NIV), "I am going to send you what my Father has promised; but stay in the city until you have been clothed with power from on high." Therefore, global leaders must think like Christ and strive to adapt to a "global mindset, global entrepreneurship (Cabrera and Unruh 2012), and surrender with humility to move beyond the status quo.

CHAPTER 5
Great Commission: The Apostle Paul's Approach to Inclusiveness and Alignment

God's decision to scatter people globally in the story of Babel affirmed His intent pre-sin, and the strategy of the Great Commission was useful because it was simple and involved preaching the Word, establishing churches, and appointing elders to rule local churches (Bishop 2014).

The day of Pentecost marked the beginning of the church. It also established the stage for the type of leadership courage that would prove to be invaluable to the spreading of the Gospel across Judea, Samaria, and into the world (Acts 8). Paul's contribution to the spread of the Gospel was undeniably successful. Through his leadership acumen, sound strategic thinking, and the empowerment of the Holy Spirit, his leadership transcended cultural differences and transformed the lives of many. His conversion marked the beginning of a radical movement—arguing that "through grace in Christ, all persons are chosen, not just those raised under Jewish law" (Marquant 1997). Paul led with excellence, purpose, principles, and passion through others. It is palpable that the concept of leadership has been evolving from the time of Paul's era and continues to progress with time and with different scholars' interpretations. Amid changes and global demands for leadership, the characteristics that made leaders "good" in the early Christian communities remain constant in modern times.

The apostle Paul may not have been one of the church leaders in the upper room on the day of Pentecost; he was nevertheless one of the pioneers that made the most impact in the spreading of the Gospel. He carried out the Great Commission of Mark 16:15–18: "Go into all the world and preach the Gospel to all creation. Whoever believes and is baptized will be saved, but whoever does not believe will be condemned. And these signs will accompany those who believe: In my name, they will drive out demons; they will speak in new tongues; they will pick up snakes with their hands; and when they drink deadly poison, it will not hurt them at all; they will place their hands on sick people, and they will get well." Paul's missionary career epitomizes the account of Mark 16:15–18.

As a young man, Paul expended a lot of energy pursuing Christians for their newfound faith to hinder the movement. He affirms in Galatians 1:13, "There was simply no limit to the way I persecuted the church of God in my attempts to destroy it." He then had a dramatic conversion and began spreading the Gospel even more enthusiastically than he once persecuted its followers (Holley 2011). His cultural versatility was beneficial to his leadership and helped him to build trust among his followers and leaders alike. His qualifications for the task came from a combination of his education and the leading of the Holy Spirit (Acts 22:3). As a native of Tarsus located in the Roman province of Cilicia, Paul was culturally competent by nature. He preached with the weight of experience and with the force of repentance and conversion (Holley 2011), reaching across culture lines to plant churches throughout Asia Minor and the Greek peninsula.

He spent approximately fifteen to twenty years of apostolic ministry resulted in "clusters of church plants in four Roman Empire provinces…he spent considerable time evangelizing in several cities around the northwestern rim of the Mediterranean," immediately following his conversion on the road to Damascus (Culbertson 2017, 48–49). Paul was able to carry the Gospel across borders to the Gentiles and was "drawn to the frontiers where the Gospel had not yet been proclaimed" (Culbertson 2017). He added that "Paul seemed driven to do what the Great Commission calls God's people to do."

Strategies and Principles Employed by the Apostle Paul

Paul's strategies are difficult to compare to today's anthropocentric model, which relies heavily on committees, workshops, retreats, and conferences (Jonkman 2017) to carry out initiatives. Nevertheless, his strategy could be well defined as one a flexible method of procedure, developed under the guidance of the Holy Spirit, and subject to His direction and control. He was known to plan his journeys purposely, selected specific strategic points at which to plant his churches, and then actually carried out his designs (Jonkman 2011–2017 cited Bennett 1980, 138).

It could be interpreted that Paul utilized mixed methods to position himself for success and concentrated on culture relativity and leadership style, such as the Leader-Member Exchange Theory, for its collective nature.

Northouse expounds that Leader-Member Exchange Theory is "a relationship-based approach to leadership that focuses on two-way—dyadic relationship," an approach that paves the way for the right interactions between leaders and followers. As such, Paul was successful in moving the Gospel cross-culturally for he inspired people who came from different cultural traditions, to trust his messages and becoming a follower of Jesus as a result. He was successful in building a community of believers and Christian leaders like Timothy, Silas, Titus, Epaphroditus, the Ephesian elders.

Another aspect of the Leader-Member Exchange Theory is inclusion. As a leader who works so fearlessly to include the Gentiles to the Christian faith, "Paul was able to reach a broad audience and endorsed the inclusion of all people in the Church. He spread the Christian message across the Mediterranean during the first century CE and devoted his time, ensuring the Word of Christ was consistent among all the cities. Through written correspondence, he speaks as an apostle of Christ, suggesting ways in which the communities can address specific issues with which they faced" (Casey 2012, 2). He imitated the values of

Jesus, who came to restore humanity as a whole and offered power and dominion to all who believe (Mark 16) through ongoing communication and relationship with the Holy Spirit.

For Paul, the Great Commission was not about his power or abilities. His mission was ultimately to build productive relationships through mutual consensus. His leadership was relational, personal, and directed toward the good of others. He took active steps to foster relationships, using his letters as a means of being present with those from whom he was physically absent. He made it a point to not just preach the Gospel but to establish sound relationships, relationships in which he was a genuine participant (Smith 2014). As a result, Paul was keen on considering the context to help detangle culture paradoxes and work effectively among different settings. Paul arguably was known as "the second most significant figure of the early church; a man whose blinding conversion and organizational genius changed the ancient world; and whose letters make up one-third of the New Testament, and who walked 10,000 miles through the Roman Empire" (Marquand 1997).

Moreover, Paul grasped his mission "to preach the Gospel to the Gentiles" and consequently narrowed his efforts to where he would be more successful: cultural location and his commitment to integrate and learn in the culture; natural environment and resources. He used his abilities to contribute to the local economy and used his resources to support his mission; flexible but yet uncompromising message. His attributes and the principles he lived by symbolized characteristics of global leadership. During his missionary journeys, Jonkman (2017) summarizes Paul's approach as follows: He concentrated on four of the most populous and prosperous provinces, Galatia, Asia, Macedonia, and Achaia with the Holy Spirit guiding him along the way. He established centers Christian in the important cities, where the Gospel might then spread to the provinces (Acts 19:10). He began in the synagogues and targeted the Jews first (Romans 16:1). In Acts 13:46, however, he turned his back to the Jews and went to the Gentiles for the Jews "rejected" his message. He maintained strong connection to his home church and solicited support when he required (Romans 15:15). He planted churches, made use of his fellow workers, became all things to all people, and communicated an unchanging message.

Obstacles and Challenges that Paul Encountered and Overcame

Although Paul was able to build trust among many during his travel, he demonstrated the Gospel of Jesus in words and deeds. He nevertheless faced fierce opposition and challenges throughout his ministry—from internal and external persecutions, trials, and physical sufferings, to the rigors of ministry, his quality of life during his ministry. His absolute conviction in Jesus as the Messiah and the lengths he went to affirm that conviction was not received positively (Marquand 1997).

The apostle Paul committed himself to long, grueling hours of work as a tentmaker. He did this to avoid being a financial burden on the church at which he was ministering (2 Corinthians 11). He clarifies, "We put no stumbling block in anyone's path so that our ministry will not be discredited. Instead, as servants of God we commend ourselves in every way: in high endurance; in troubles, hardships and distresses; beatings, imprisonments and riots; in hard work, sleepless nights and hunger" (2 Corinthians 6:3–10) for the sake of the Gospel. Paul did not want to: (1) hinder men and women from accepting the Gospel and (2) do anything that discredited the message he preached (Reed 2016; 2 Corinthians 6:3–13 commentaries). In this example, Paul practiced one of the characteristics of today's exemplary leadership: he modeled the way by behaving in ways to showcase the focus on the mission to preach the Gospel to the Gentiles without any hindrances.

He recognized that to gain commitment and achieve the highest standards, it was necessary to model the behaviors he expected of others—aligning his actions with shared values (Kouzes and Posner 2012, 16).

For the sake of the Gospel, Paul was arrested and was beaten to the point of death. In 2 Corinthians 1:8–10, he explains the enormous pressure he had been subjected to. "We do not want you to be uninformed, brothers and sisters, about the troubles we experienced in the province of Asia. We were under great pressure, far beyond our ability to endure, so that we despaired of life itself. Indeed, we felt we had received a sentence of death. But this happened that we might not rely on ourselves but on God, who raises the dead." Paul endured countless physical ordeal—"being flogged many times," as he described in 2 Corinthians 11:25–28:

> I have worked much harder, been in prison more frequently, been flogged more severely, and been exposed to death again and again. Five times I received from the Jews the forty lashes minus one. Three times I was beaten with rods, once I was pelted with stones, three times I was shipwrecked, I spent a night and a day in the open sea, I have been constantly on the move. I have been in danger from rivers, in danger from bandits, in danger from my fellow Jews, in danger from Gentiles; in danger in the city, in danger in the country, in danger at sea; and in danger from false believers. I have labored and toiled and have often gone without sleep; I have known hunger and thirst and have often gone without food; I have been cold and naked. Besides everything else, I face daily the pressure of my concern for all the churches.

Great leadership in today's global setting requires what Aristotle refers to as the "first virtue: courage" because it makes all of the other virtues possible. Paul was never afraid, even under constant persecutions and threats to his life. He continued to stay the course in the face of dangers that he has encountered and deprivations he underwent in the line of carrying the Gospel to the Gentiles and others (2 Corinthians 11 and 12 commentaries), extending the reach of the church and teaching leaders to take on the challenges of the local churches.

Moreover, Paul experienced many conflicts—both internally (with the religious leaders) and externally (challenging the disciples and confronting the churches for practices he thought were inconsistent with the Gospel of Jesus Christ). For example, the tension over what exactly should be required of new converts, or more specifically, how Judaism fits into the Christian movement, caused Paul ongoing problems in several cities where he planted churches, as in Corinth (Holley 2011). Part of the issues Paul had in regard of the new converts stemmed from the fact that Paul was not part of the "original" disciples of Jesus but was known to have had the authority that "came from faith, from an experience with the risen Christ that isn't so different from any of us" (Holley 2011). Paul's unwillingness to serve any authority but Christ put him at odds with the official church (Marquand 1997) and hated by many.

CHAPTER 6
A Paradigm Shift

Leadership and work continue to dominate our world today as it has been since the beginning of time. Scholars and leaders alike continue to seek creative and innovative ways to redefine leadership behaviors aimed to produce excellence, minimizing the apparent missing link—love, the recipe for all that exists on earth. Through love, a relationship is developed and maintained. Love is the prerequisite for building sustainable cultures—that change and transform people for it is concerned with emotions, values, ethics, standards, and long-term goals—to satisfying people's needs while treating them as human beings (Northouse 2013). Although love is not a word of expression, you hear it uttered in the office hallways or conference rooms. And yet, it has a strong influence on workplace outcomes (Barsade and O'Neil 2014). They posit "that employees who felt they worked in a loving, caring culture reported higher levels of satisfaction and teamwork. They showed up to work more often" (Administrative Science Quarterly survey, "What's Love Got to Do With It?").

When leaders lead with love, their focus is on self-transformation, self-development, as well as others to become self-aware. Highly self-aware leaders identify strongly with being a leader and are highly self-efficacious are more likely to be effective leaders (Day and Dragoni 2015). Their ultimate goal is to leave a legacy rather than self-promotion. They invest time and resources to enhance their capabilities and enrich the increasingly dynamic, complex, and demanding environment (Uhl-Bien and Arena 2017).

Moreover, leaders who lead with love can engage better with a diverse workforce. As a result of today's global culture, many organizations are making employee engagement a priority for their leaders. The requirement for leaders to engage with a wide range of stakeholders, including suppliers, customers, government and industry regulators, or employees from diverse multicultural, ethnic, and religious backgrounds is precedent. As a result of these challenges, companies seek to develop leaders who can influence people different from themselves in numerous compound ways, assert Fry and Egel (2017). Fry and Egel believe one of the methods is for organizations to invest and commit to sustainable development or "greenwashing," whereby disinformation is disseminated by an organization to present an environmentally responsible public image. They also believe that "solutions for a sustainable, even flourishing world require a new model of leadership that fosters a sustainability mindset—"spiritual leadership." Spiritual leadership places social and environmental sustainability, at least on par with profitability and maximizing shareholder wealth. As a result, they conclude this model will make it possible to uphold social well-being and quality of life without degrading the ecological systems upon which life depends. The two believe that "spirituality" is concerned with qualities of the human spirit and that intangible reality at the core of personality, the animating life principle, or life-breath that alerts us to look for the most profound dimension of human experience.

Another missing link in the pursuit of excellence, which is the necessity for leaders to possess a global mindset, a mental competency that enables global leaders to work across culture successfully. Global mindset has three essential components (refer to "Global Mindset Capitals"): (1) psychological capital/personality trait that enables a person to open up to things that are different; (2) intellect capital/ability to learn other trends from diverse cultures; and (3) social capital/ability to build cross-culture relationships. These three components must be mastered to some extent to enable global leaders to work across cultures (Cabrera and Unruh 2012).

Rhinesmith (1992, 64) argues that people with global mindsets tend to drive for the bigger, broader picture. They accept life as a balance of contradictory forces, trust organizational processes rather than structure, value diversity, are comfortable with surprises and ambiguity, and seek to be open to themselves and others. Thus, according to Rhinesmith, Global Mindset entails high levels of cognitive capabilities, especially scanning and information processing capabilities, as well as the ability to balance competing realities and demands and to appreciate cultural diversity.

Leaders who pursue excellence demonstrate strong ethical behaviors, foster a sense of connection and belonging, show openness to new ideas and foster organizational learning, and nurtures growth (Giles 2016). They are committed "to mobilize others to want to make extraordinary things happen"—personally and spiritually (Kouzes and Posner 2012) and are mainly dedicated to upholding practices that "transform values into actions, visions into realities, obstacles into innovations, separateness into solidarity, and risks into rewards." Together, Kouzes and Posner identify these practices as (1) model the way, (2) inspire a shared vision, (3) challenge the process, (4) enable others to act, and (5) encourage the heart.

The apostle Paul demonstrates both characteristics: love and a global mindset. He led in "love" for both the work he was doing as an apostle and the people he sought after. His love empowered him to model the way in aligning his actions with shared values—which enabled him to be productive and successful in the spreading of the Gospel and rebuking his fellow brothers and sisters in Christ as necessary. For example, Paul addressed various concerns among the members of the faith community in 1 Thessalonians 2:4–9:

> But as we have been approved by God to be entrusted with the gospel, even so we speak, not as pleasing men, but God who tests our hearts. For neither at any time did we use flattering words, as you know, nor a cloak for covetousness—God is witness. Nor did we seek glory from men, either from you or from others, when we might have made

demands as apostles of Christ. But we were gentle among you, just as a nursing mother cherishes her own children. So, affectionately longing for you, we were well pleased to impart to you not only the gospel of God, but also our own lives, because you had become dear to us. For you remember, brethren, our labor and toil; for laboring night and day, that we might not be a burden to any of you, we preached to you the gospel of God.

As uttered by Kouzes and Posner (2012), one of the actions of modeling the way is to "let your values guide you at all times. Meaning allowing 'your values to influence every aspect of your life: your moral judgments, your responses to others, your commitments to personal and organizational goals'" (p. 49). Paul exemplifies his values to the Corinthians, who lived in southern Greece, by refusing compensations as he acknowledges in 1 Corinthians 9:12–18: "But, we did not use this right. On the contrary, we put up with anything rather than hinder the gospel of Christ."

His success was based solely on his love for God, which empowered him to put his own interest unimportant for the well-being of others.

His love causes him to remain obedient and faithful until the end of his journey. He endured hardship but yet found the strength to stay the course. He affirms, "I have fought the good fight, I have finished the race, I have kept the faith. Now there is in store for me the crown of righteousness, which the Lord, the righteous Judge, will award to me on that day—and not only to me but also to all who have longed for His appearing" (2 Timothy 4:7–8).

"Waiting for His appearance" as a gardener awaits his plants. The Lord God placed man in the garden to watch over it, using one of the garden principles, love: to becoming "fruitful" and to "multiply. The love of the gardener for the work he or she does is time-consuming, one that requires love and proper planning, that includes abiding by the fundamentals, such as the right timing, light, good soil, planting time, and adequate spacing between plants. Becoming knowledgeable about what makes each plant grows—plant's spacing needs and developing habits. For example, some vegetables grow upright; others trail along the ground, and still, others have a vining habit, such as tomatoes, cucumbers, peas, and beans; trellises encourage upward growth (Chaker 2010).

Through our day-to-day work, we have an opportunity to fulfill the Great Commission and transform people's lives in the processes. We can foster a culture of trust that includes all as opposed to one that suits our selfish ambitions. Jesus used the marketplace to model the need for work to be used as a vehicle for successful relationships. We are the body of Christ on earth, and when we do our work right, it is the work of God, the work of Christ we are doing, empowered by the Spirit, inspired by the example of Christ, guided by the Word which led the apostle Paul to his suffering (Witherington III 2011).

The propensity for excellence in leadership must include a love of work and people from a global perspective. We are called to go into the world—an inclusive approach that requires the love of work and the love of people to be successful. The Great Commission incorporates that through work, God's leaders would be able to reach a "world in which God reached down to the poor and helpless, touching the untouchables, healing the sick and broken, and reconciling people, society, and all creation to the Creator. It is this work of the loving touch, healing, and combining that I and others call "kingdom work" (Lingenfelter 2008).

There is a dire need for leaders to incorporate love in their practices in particular in today's interconnectedness of the world. Today's success of leaders is dependent on their abilities to respond to and adapt to people from different cultural settings, "ensuring that everyone is aligned through the process of affirming shared values—uncovering, reinforcing, and holding one another accountable" to extend and sustain love (Kouzes and Posner 2012). Love is universal and is the antidote against prejudices and biases. Love combines with sound leadership practices, create paths that align dreams of the leader with the people's dream, argue Kouzes and Posner. Using the "I Have a Dream" speech of one of the most admired and prolific leaders, Martin Luther King Jr., Kouzes and Posner (2012) explain the possible outcome of such combination in the following observations:

> He appealed to common interests.
>
> He talked about traditional values of family, church, and country.
>
> It was vivid. He used a lot of images and word pictures. You could see the example.
>
> People could relate to the examples. They were familiar.
>
> His references were credible. It's hard to argue against the Constitution or the Bible.
>
> He mentioned children—something we can all relate to.
>
> It was personal. He mentioned his own children, but it wasn't just his kids because he also talked about everyone's children.
>
> He knew his audience.
>
> He made geographical references to places the people in the audience could relate to.
>
> He included everybody: different parts of the country, all ages, both sexes, major religions several times.
>
> He used a lot of repetition: for example, saying "I have a dream," and "Let freedom ring" several times.
>
> He talked about the same ideas many times but in different ways. (p. 137)

Dr. King's speech characteristics incorporate both the love for his work/mission and the love for the people. He was "selfless. He exemplified the features of the Garden culture—love that led to sacrifice. By sacrificing, he demonstrated that he was not in it for himself; instead, he had the interests of others at heart" (Kouzes and Posner et al. 2004). God exhibited love in the pursuit and consequent actions following the fall of man with Adam and Eve. He chastised and punished them severely; nevertheless, He showed great compassion. "He made garments of skin for Adam and his wife and clothed them" before driving them out of the garden of Eden (Genesis 3:21–24).

Moreover, God remembered Noah and all the wild animals and the livestock that were with him in the ark, and He sent a wind over the earth, and the waters receded after wickedness entered the world (Genesis 6:1–4). The ultimate display of love for humanity was realized in the coming of the Messiah. He came and died to redeem humanity from the fall. These acts of love help leaders to champion a culture of compassion, exemplify passion that attracts people, and creates lots of enthusiasm, excitement, and zeal for their cause (Kouzes and Posner et al. 2004).

Chapter 7
Bringing It All Together: The Need to Go Back to the Beginning

The term *leadership*, as well as any other created being and processes, came to existence from the beginning. In Psalm 24, David points out convincingly that the "earth belongs to the Lord's, and the fullness thereof; the world, and they that dwell therein. For He hath founded it upon the seas and established it upon the floods." And Colossians 1:16 states, "For by Him all things were created, in heaven and on earth, visible and invisible, whether thrones or dominions or rulers or authorities—all things were created through Him and for Him." Distorted views about the term leadership, the nature of work, and long-standing opinions about the separation of state and church practices often dominate the world stage. However, they fail to produce standard values that most businesses and leaders alike are willing to adopt and implement.

The quest to redefine what God has created has caused disagreements, dismays, segregations of different groups and cultures, discrimination, the pursuit to dominate the world stage, overlooking the true meaning and purpose of creation. The lust of the flesh, the lust of the eyes and pride caused Adam and Eve to disobey God, and humanity was hit as a result. The result of their disobedience was immediately apparent right after their encounter with Satan. The man begins to use God-given creativity for personal gains, power, and greed as opposed to obeying God's command entirely.

Partial obedience or blatant forms of disobedience become the norm. The first Roman emperor to claim conversion to Christianity was Constantine, who was regarded by the Orthodox Church as Saint Constantine the Great, asserts Shcall (1995). Shcall posed the question: "When you hear his name (Constantine), do you think of the power and brutality of the Roman Empire, or do you think of the founding of formalized Christianity? Was Constantine good, bad, a mixture?" If the truth be told, Constantine saw himself as God and behaved as such for personal gains and power throughout his reign. Shcall expounds his insolence as outlined below:

> Constantine gained political power the way most ancients did, through warfare and murder. His troops admired him and they proclaimed him as Augustus of the West at his father's death, as he served with them in Britain. Other political pretenders reduced his title to Caesar, but he ruled over Britain, Gaul, and Spain with one of the largest armies in the Roman Empire. When he captured two kings and the soldiers of the Franks, he fed them to beasts in the amphitheater in Trier. He married the daughter of a political rival, Maximian, with the promise to protect the man's son, but he was in another location, conveniently, when the man was attacked. Later he arranged for the suicide of the same rival. In another battle for dominance, Constantine painted the sign of the Christian cross on his soldiers' shields and created a battle standard with the same symbol, convinced, perhaps by a dream or vision, that this would make him victorious. Once he defeated his remaining rivals, Constantine became the sole Emperor of the Roman Empire. His final battle was permeated with religious language; Constantine presented himself as a savior of the Christians in the Roman East.

It was clear from early on that Christianity was created to last. For Jesus said to Peter in Matthew 16:18, "And on this rock, I will build my church, and the gates of Hades will not overcome it." Against fierce persecutions and hard times, harassment, oppression, and killing for their beliefs, the movement persisted, and its growth was persistent. Before the reign of Constantine, there were examples and substantiation of Christians being arrested, beheaded, imprisoned, beaten, tortured, murdered, and executed. The movement did not need a savior. As stated by Shcall,

> Christianity developed well throughout the Mediterranean in the three centuries before Constantine. There were periods of persecution. Often, brave Christian martyrs expanded pagan respect for Christianity with an accompanying growth of Christian communities. The communities themselves were attractions for people who wanted to help others or people who needed help. They were instrumental in the growth of social services for people who had had no other place to turn. Thus, Christianity provided a new religion of hope *and* a system of compassionate social services. Its appeal continues, with the recent rapid growth of Christian communities in Africa and South America.

Jesus warns His disciples before He ascended in several passages beginning with Matthew 10:22: "You will be persecuted by everyone because of me, but the one who stands firm to the end will be saved." Second Corinthians 4:9 states, "Persecuted, but not abandoned, struck down, but not destroyed."

Nevertheless, Constantine is known to have accomplished various positive things for the Christian faith and asserted himself as a model leader for the Christians. Constantine, as Shcall (1995) puts it, "built the Church of the Holy Sepulcher at the purported site of Jesus' tomb, which became the holiest site in Christendom.

During his reign, he created many basilicas, repaired churches, and saw that Sunday was designated as a day of rest for all citizens. He promoted Christians into political offices. Constantine decided his capital was to be moved to Byzantium. He did extensive building in this city, then renamed it Constantinople. This "new city" was said to be safeguarded by relics of the True Cross, the Rod of Moses, and other holy relics. Figures of the old gods were replaced or assimilated into Christian symbolism. Constantine himself was baptized into the Christian faith right before his death." He, unfortunately, became known as a model that his successors held as standards. Those standards had great implications for the broader parts. "If the emperor must be the Man of God, then anyone who opposed him necessarily became demonized, literally—cast" (Drake 2016).

In 1 Kings 19:16, 2 Kings 10:36, and other Old Testament passages, the story of Jehu son of Nimshi, king over Israel, is a replica of Constantine's account—the quest for political power. He used religion for personal gains and to sustain greed and self-promotions. Jehu was anointed by Elijah with a clear mission to "put to death any who escape the sword of Hazael" (1 Kings 20:17). However, Jehu's personal interest obstructed his obedience to God's direct command. He instead partially obeyed and destroyed Baal worship in Israel and did not turn away from the sins of Jeroboam son of Nephat, which he had caused Israel to commit—the worship of the golden calves at Bethel and Dan—and was not careful to keep the law of the Lord (2 Kings 10:27–31). It is believed that Jehu's motives for not destroying the golden calves in Bethel and Dan may have been more political than spiritual (NIV cross-reference Application Study Bible). Accordingly, justification is as follows:

1. If Jehu had destroyed the golden calves, his people would have traveled to the temple in Jerusalem, in rival southern kingdom, and worshiped there—which is why Jeroboam set them up in the first place, according to 1 Kings 12:25–33's account.

2. Baal worship was associated with the dynasty of Ahad, so it was politically advantageous to destroy Baal. The golden

calves, on the other hand, had a longer history in the northern kingdom and were valued by all political factions.

3. Baal worship was anti-God, but the golden calves were thought by many to be visible representations of God Himself even though God's law stated clearly that such worship was idolatrous (Exodus 20:3–6 NIV, ASB).

The truth is we were all created like God with His characteristics. One of which is "dominion"—to be man in charge and to rule over all living things. Man was empowered to be successful to build high-performing cultures, relationships, businesses, and projects. Hebrew 2:6–8 raises the question, "What is mankind that you are mindful of them, a son of man that you care for him? You made them a little lower than the angels; you crowned them with glory and honor and put everything under their feet." Dominion to rule and subdue the earth and all therein was given to mankind to lead successfully in all aspects. The following scriptures support that notion:

> And to put on the new man who has been created in God's image—in righteousness and holiness that comes from truth. (Ephesians 4:24)

> Dear friends, we are God's children now, and what we will be has not yet been revealed. We know that whenever it is revealed we will be like him, because we will see him just as he is. (1 John 2:3)

> If I then, your Lord and Teacher, have washed your feet, you too ought to wash one another's feet. Everyone will know by this that you are my disciples—if you have love for one another. (John 13:14, 35)

The characteristics of God as seen throughout the Bible are applicable standards for successful life and business practices.

Nevertheless, mankind has a tendency of contesting creation standards by defying God's approved ways for success.

Dominion over all things created was in bold display in the garden through labor and the seamless working relationship between God, the Creator, and Adam, assigned leader. There was no need for "rain on earth, but streams came up from the earth and watered the whole surface of the ground," all trees that were pleasing to the eye and good for food. There was a river watering the garden that flowed from Eden, according to Genesis 2. Man lacks nothing in a culture established by God Himself. God was visibly engaged in supporting the development of that culture and effectively, motivated Adam to do the same.

Sins did not change the love and plan of God for man. His salvation plan was put in action immediately (Genesis 3:15), and the leadership appointments increased with each passing time. He chose Noah, who found favor in His eyes, and assigned him the ark project: to build a large boat that would withstand the Noachian to protect the remnant of humanity (Genesis 6:8–22).

From the house of Pharaoh, He handpicked Moses and tasked him to lead the "deliverance" project as outlined in Exodus 3:1–11:

> Moses, Moses...I am the God of Abraham, the God of Isaac, and the God of Jacob. I have indeed seen the misery of my people in Egypt. I have heard them crying out because of their slave drivers, and I am concerned about their suffering. So, I have come down to rescue them from the hand of the Egyptians and to bring them up out of that land into a good and spacious land, a land flowing with milk and honey. So now, go. I am sending you to Pharaoh to bring my people out of Egypt.

Moreover, to keep the vow He made to David, God allowed Solomon to begin and complete the temple project:

> The Lord God as chosen my son Solomon to sit on the throne of the kingdom of the Lord over Israel...He said to me Solomon, your son is the one who will build my house and my courts, for I have chosen him to be my son, and I will be his father. (1 Chronicles 28:5–7)

Additionally, the Lord God selected Nehemiah and empowered him to take on the wall project:

> I went to Jerusalem, and after staying there three days I set out during the night with a few men. I had not told anyone what my God had put in my heart to do for Jerusalem. Come, let us rebuild the wall of Jerusalem, and we will no longer be in disgrace. (Nehemiah 2:11–18)

God selects Moses, Joshua, Noah, Nehemiah, and Joseph to lead and fulfill His plans and to highlight His desires for leaders to lead for the sole purpose of His glory. God is a worker and is introduced as such in Genesis 1:1. Unfortunately, the world sees work as a self-fulfillment interest, which is a direct contradiction of why work was created. God wants us to use business and work to fulfill His purpose on earth; such a mandate can only be accomplished using the business environment as a vehicle. Furthermore, the first entrepreneurs, Cain and Able, are also introduced to us at the beginning of Genesis (Genesis 4). One was a farmer (Cain works the soil [Genesis 4:2]), and the other, a shepherd (Able kept the flocks [Genesis 4:2]).

Moreover, it is not a coincidence that most of Jesus's twelve original disciples were identified as businessmen. Six were fishermen operating established businesses in Galilee, most notably Peter, James, and John. Matthew was a taxman with an office in bustling

Capernaum. Another key follower, Luke, was known to be a practicing physician (NIV Study Bible).

Likewise, Jesus was raised in a family business that supported a family of at least nine and was more than a mere carpenter. Business in the Bible as noted by Gray (2013) referenced that many of Jesus's public ministry appearances seem to have been in the marketplace and workplace. There are believed to be about fifty parables told, and approximately thirty-four of them can be described as having a business, finance, or workplace content as the illustration. God intended to create a world in which work, business, and ministry coexisted. The separation between work, business, and ministry is the direct result of sin. Jesus came to repair the damage that was introduced by Satan in the garden so we can live a life that exemplifies God's purpose for leaders. He gives leaders knowledge and wisdom to yield fruit in all aspects.

It is also important to notice all of the leaders chosen by God had no prior experiences to draw from. However, the selected leaders embodied different leadership abilities for success. One of such is creativity and innovation. The chosen leaders were tasked to develop strategic plans to accomplish a goal which required the ability to gather resources, i.e., materials, people; they had to design and implement plans and processes to achieve their goals. For example, Solomon was tasked to build the "Temple of God." As part of his creativity, he sent "his envoys to Hiram king of Tyre," an unlikely source, to inform him about his plan to build the temple of the Lord on behalf of his father David (NIV Study Bible). First Kings 5:6 states that Solomon requested that the king "give orders that cedars of Lebanon be cut for him." He said, "My men will work with yours, and I will pay you for your men whatever wages you set. You know that we have no one skilled in felling timber as the Sidonians." The Bible confirms that a deal was reached between the two kings, and Solomon, as a result, exchanged wheat and made other deals for the cost of wood and labor.

Additionally, through divine abilities and skills needed to all the leading individuals, Nehemiah was seen as an innovative leader who secretly inspected the "wall during the night with a few men" before deciding to announce his plans to the residents of Jerusalem (Neh. 2:11–17).

Keller (2012) states that "the Bible begins talking about work as soon as it begins talking about anything—that is how important and basic it is." He further states that "work was not a necessary evil that came into the picture later or something human beings were created to do that was beneath the great God himself." In other words, business and work are at the core of the Bible with leadership included as the vehicle to create excellent and satisfying work (Keller 2012). Therefore, throughout the Old Testament, we see a pattern of God's plan for His creation in action, using these early leaders as role models to display His ideas of leadership and to accomplish His goals. God is the author and finisher of all artistic exploits. God summoned Noah, Moses, Solomon, Nehemiah, Joshua, as He directs all leaders to work and experience the goodness of work.

Principles to Experience Good Work as Commanded by God

Giving the long-established pattern of work and the continued quest to define leadership in a consensus model, there is a need to go back to the garden's mandate: one that is inclusive, with global intent, and accessible to all. Moreover, work, as it was created, was defined as "good." It was "as much a basic human need as food, beauty, rest, friendship, prayer, and sexuality; it is not simply medicine but food for our soul. Without meaningful work, we sense significant inner loss and emptiness" (Keller 2012). The gaps between godly practices, business, and work are wider even among Christians. Leading work are often leaders with personal agendas who care only about their own needs as opposed to the glory of God. Man continues to invent more creative ways to disobey the commands of God and practices thereof. There are widespread views among Christians that work, business, and faith are mutually exclusive: and that (1) work is a matter of practical reality having little to do with religion with the possible exception of some moral and ethical values. At the same time, the other is (2) merely a matter of private or personal belief.

As established, leadership, work, and business are integral parts of scriptures and are included in various scripture passages:

1. Isaiah 43:37 states, "Everyone who is called by my name, whom I created for my glory, whom I formed and made."
2. Ephesians 3:9–10 substantiates, "And to bring to light for everyone what is the plan of the mystery hidden for ages in God who created all things so that through the church the manifold wisdom of God might now be made known to the rulers and authorities in the heavenly places."
3. Ephesians 2:10 argues, "For we are His workmanship, created in Christ Jesus for good works, which God prepared beforehand, that we should walk in them."
4. Revelation 4:11 suggests, "Thou art worthy, O Lord, to receive glory and honor and power: for thou hast created all things, and for thy pleasure, they are and were created."

Success begins with one's ability to change. The criteria for leadership and organizational successes (as Jesus described to Nicodemus in John 3:1–21) are dependent upon a leader's ability to adapt and acquire a new "heart." Jesus, who was both Man and God, told Nicodemus, a leader and a Pharisee, who was a member of the Jewish ruling council, that "no one can see the Kingdom of God unless they are born again." Having a new perspective is what Jesus came to reveal to His disciples. He came to create a culture in which leaders are open to change and to accept the need for change. He challenged them to be poor in spirit and to develop an attitude of humility using the Beatitudes He gives, which is also known as the Sermon on the Mount (see appendix B). The concept of change was foreign to Nicodemus because he couldn't relate to what Jesus was saying. "Despite Jesus' efforts to open Nicodemus's eyes, Nicodemus remains nonplussed. He does not reject what Jesus tells him but instead fails to understand what Jesus could have been saying. There is great irony as Nicodemus, the 'teacher of Israel' and 'ruler of the Jews' is unable to grasp even earthly things, let alone heavenly things" (Johnson 2013).

Comparably to Nicodemus, successful organizations are often led by leaders who understand change and can prepare their organizations to respond to change. Tichy (1997) refers to leaders who embrace change as "winning leaders." Tichy argues, those leaders don't shy away from the future nor globalization. They are about "building an organization that responds to customers' demands today and can do so again tomorrow and the next day. They are constantly looking ahead. They watch the horizon to spot impending changes in the marketplace so they can develop ideas and structures that will allow the organization to respond efficiently and effectively."

Acquiring a new perspective requires that leaders (1) accept the basic tenets that God is Sovereign overall; (2) believe in the truth of the Gospel; (3) believe that God created all things and created man in his image, that He sent His Son to redeem all things that had been broken; (4) believe that God has a purpose for all workers and leaders who could make a positive difference in the world—rejecting the competitive, win-at-all-costs workplace culture and accepting to be led by the fruit of the Spirit (see appendix C) to bear fruit and experience sustainable result.

Jesus's coaching model is still applicable today. He called the twelve disciples and equipped them through various hands-on experience and coaching actions. He sends them two by two and gives them power and authority to do the same as He taught them.

> Jesus had 12 disciples. He coached (discipled) them. He could have taken a different approach by merely meeting the needs of hundreds of thousands of people. After all, everyone needed His life-changing touch. But Jesus understood the importance of leaving a legacy of having lasting results. Because of this, He invested in His disciples by giving them time and focused attention. His one and an only winning strategy for passing on His life to the next generation was to spend three years disciplining His disciples. And in the end, He sent them out to do as He had

done, to "make disciples of all the nations. (St Clair [2007] cites Matthew 28:19)

Why Is Coaching Important and Beneficial Today?

Coaching is about change for both, the coachee and the coach (willingness to change and be born anew as Jesus explained to Nicodemus). Before a coach can encourage others to change, he/she must be flexible to change and willing to be compliant and lead by example. Coaching is all about embracing something new and disruption to the "status quo" that brings new habits grounded on strategic goals. Hebrew 12:1 confirms, "Since we are surrounded by such a great cloud of witnesses, let us throw off everything that hinders and the sin that so easily entangles, and let us run with perseverance the race marked out for us." Just as in the time of Jesus, the need to make leadership development relevant to the current business has to become a priority because high performance is no longer an option but a requirement for the survival of both individuals and organizations. Leadership skills grounded on biblical characteristics and the performance thereof are needed now more than ever.

Coaching, as Jesus established, has the potential to help leaders to build relationships that can help them to guide others effectively into increased competence, commitment, and confidence. The ability to reach across boundaries and culture line is what causes leaders to be successful in aligning people, processes, and culture. At its core, coaching is a proactive concept, one that disrupts the status quo and foster developmental change in people looking to move to higher fulfillment. Successful leadership occurs when leaders can create shared vision through productive relationships and assimilation with the people they lead, when they are successful and able to develop long-term goals, and all the while bypassing the pressures of today to focus on performance. Lastly, those leaders can overcome the challenge of "balancing current operational needs as oppose to looking at the long-term perspective of growth and development of staff and business practice."

When combined with coaching, leadership development helps equip leaders to acquire the aptitude to translate the vision of future opportunity into coherent organizational strategies, unleashing human potential to execute consistently on strategic priorities. They are also able to adapt to external change and internal conditions (refers to coaching with a game plan, appendix D). Those leaders are more likely to reap the full performance potential of their organizations and have the potential to impact others globally in the process.

Additionally, coaching is about caring for others, as Jesus did. The account of Matthew 14:13–21 is an example of how Jesus responded to the need of the people with care and compassion:

> When it was evening, the disciples came to him and said, "This is a lonely place, and the day is now over; send the crowds away to go into the villages and buy food for themselves..." taking the five loaves and the two fish he looked up to heaven, and blessed, and broke and gave the loaves to the disciples, and the disciples gave them to the crowds... And those who ate were about five thousand men, besides women and children.

The question that all leaders ought to ask themselves is how much do you care about the people you lead, says Goldsmith et al. (2012). Goldsmith believes that leaders set the tone. An organization will grow and thrive when leaders establish/develop high standards, display a strong belief that those standards can be achieved, and then demonstrate by your actions that you practice what you preach.

Second Corinthians 3:16–18 states that we have the propensity to transform into the image of Christ "when the veil is taken away...with open face beholding as in a glass the glory of the Lord, are changed into the same image from glory to glory, even as by the Spirit of the Lord." This passage upkeeps the need to incorporate and utilize coaching to tap into leaders and organizational growth potential. As expounded in scriptures, Moses was able to successfully lead the Israelites as a result of Jethro's coaching intervention. Exodus 18:1–24 summarizes the account of Jethro and Moses in the Old Testament that outlines insights about proper coaching. "Jethro, Moses' father-in-law wisely drew out what God was doing in Moses' life and poured in at the right moment to help him develop a plan for leading God's people in healthy ways." In this account, Jethro mentored and coached Moses by meeting with him (verse 7); taking time to find out how he was doing personally (verse 7); listening to him about the ups and downs of his journey (verse 8); asking him to probe questions (verse 15); challenging unproductive behavior (verse 17); and lastly, giving wise counsel (verses 18–23) (Roeh 2008).

When coaching is part of organizational strategy, and it's systematic, it can transform corporate culture and performance, in particular, if utilized as a part of a broader leadership development program. Increasingly, organizations incorporate coaching, in specific 360 degree feedback, using the results to indicate areas in which the leadership team might benefit from working with a coach (Michelman 2005). Coaching can improve the performance of leaders because coaching is proven as a potentially powerful means of development in its own right and can be particularly powerful when used to amplify other learning experiences (Velsor et al. 2010).

CONCLUSION

Coaching for change is imitating Jesus, following in His footsteps. Paul concedes in 1 Corinthians 11:1 the need to follow Jesus as He travels to spread the Gospel. He said, "follow my example, as I follow the example of Christ." A coach is a role model—one who leads by example and showcases humility and passion for others. "Passion leads you to excel in whatever you do," deduces Keller (2012). Keller believes that passion is to sacrifice like "Christ's passion—to sacrifice your freedom for someone else."

Change is inevitable and unavoidable. We live in an always-changing world. Technology and globalization have amplified the need for leaders to adapt to change through the teaching, passion, and empowerment of others. Jesus says in Matthew 16:24, "Whoever wants to be my disciple must deny themselves and take up their cross and follow me." Romans 12:11 affirms the need to lead with passion: "never be lacking in zeal, but keep your spiritual fervor serving the Lord. Be joyful in hope, patient in affliction, faithful in serving the Lord...share with God's people who are in need. Practice hospitality...do not be proud, but be willing to associate with people of low position. Do not be conceited."

Much work has been done over the years to define leadership in a consensus and aligned approach. However, it is evident that the concept of leadership as God's instituted it and commanded it need to take precedence over other personal and scholarly factors for the betterment of the world, society as a whole, and for the glorification of God. Leaders are to make their relationships with God, the primary value of their lives, and to obey His Word simply because it was His due (Keller 2012). Keller concludes that "man was to know, serve, and love God supremely—and when we are faithful to that design, we flourish. But when we instead chose to live for ourselves, everything begins to work backward."

Part of making a relationship with God a priority is leading with a focus on the fruit of the Spirit to create accessible and inclusive cultures. To love one another as God loves: "for God so loved the world, that He gives..." (John 3:16). Give without expecting anything in return. Lead others as Jesus did—selflessly.

As we lead, we need to get to know Him and be familiar with His model. "My sheep will know my voice," affirms John 10:20–28, "they hear my voice, and I know them, and they follow me." In order words, they put in practice garden values originated to ensure effective communication between leaders and followers, all the while modeling the way: (1) appreciate work, (2) making a global impact, (3) exemplify ethical behaviors at all times, (4) balancing power and leadership to be impactful, and (5) leading with love and compassion. Applying biblical values will result in spiritual, professional, and financial prosperity. Additionally, it will result in leadership excellence to do even greater things than these (John 14:12).

Appendix A
God's Attributes/Bright Media Foundation

Because God is a personal Spirit…
I will seek intimate fellowship with Him.
"I reach out for You. I thirst for You as parched land thirsts for rain" (Psalm 143:6).

Because God is all-powerful…
He can help me with anything.
"O Sovereign LORD! You have made the heavens and earth by Your great power. Nothing is too hard for You" (Jeremiah 32:17)!

- God has the power to create anything from nothing (Psalm 33:6–9).
- God has power to deliver (Exodus 13:3).
- God's creative power is beyond our comprehension (Job 38:1–11).
- God speaks and things happen (Psalm 29:3–9).
- His resurrection power is immeasurably great (Ephesians 1:19–20).
- His creation reflects His power (Psalm 19:1–4).
- His powerful word sustains everything (Hebrews 1:3).
- He has power over death (Revelation 1:18).
- No one can challenge what God does (Daniel 4:35).
- Reveals Himself as the almighty God (Genesis 17:1).

Because God is ever-present...

He is always with me.

"Where can I go from Your Spirit? Where can I flee from Your presence? If I go up to the heavens, You are there; if I make my bed in the depths, You are there. If I rise on the wings of the dawn, if I settle on the far side of the sea, even there Your hand will guide me, Your right hand will hold me fast. If I say, 'Surely the darkness will hide me and the light become night around me,' even the darkness will not be dark to You; the night will shine like the day, for darkness is as light to You" (Psalms 139:7–12).

- All creation is dependent upon His presence (Colossians 1:17).
- God's continual presence brings contentment (Hebrews 13:5).
- God is everywhere and no one can escape Him (Psalm 139:7–12).
- No task is too large or too difficult for Him (Jeremiah 32:17, 27).
- One cannot hide from God (Jeremiah 23:23–24).

Because God knows everything...
I will go to Him with all my questions and concerns.

"He determines the course of world events; He removes kings and sets others on the throne. He gives wisdom to the wise and knowledge to the scholars" (Daniel 2:21).

Because God is sovereign...
I will joyfully submit to His will.

> *"All the people of the earth are nothing compared to Him. He has the power to do as He pleases among the angels of heaven and with those who live on earth. No one can stop Him or challenge Him, saying, 'What do You mean by doing these things'"* (Daniel 4:35)?

- God controls time and seasons (Daniel 2:21).
- God powerfully delivered His people from Egypt (Exodus 12:29–32, 13:13–31).
- God has dominion over the affairs of people (Job 12:13–25).
- God controls nature for His purposes (Job 37:2–13).
- God chose His people to become like Christ (Romans 8:28–30).
- God chose His people before He made the world (Ephesians 1:4).
- God's eternal purpose is to make His wisdom known (Ephesians 3:10–11).
- He raises and removes rulers (Daniel 2:21).
- He has a plan for His people and will carry it out (Ephesians 1:5, 11).
- He chose His people to save and purify them (2 Thessalonians 2:13).
- He is the only Sovereign (1 Timothy 1:17, 6:15).
- The Creator looks after His creation (Psalm 104:3–32).
- The powerful Creator reduces human rulers to nothing (Isaiah 40:21–26).
- Relationship with God requires worship (John 4:24).
- God has dominion over the affairs of people (Job 12.13–25).
- God controls nature for His purposes (Job 37:2–13).
- God chose His people to become like Christ (Romans 8:28–30).

- God chose His people before He made the world (Ephesians 1:4).
- God's eternal purpose is to make His wisdom known (Ephesians 3:10–11).
- He raises and removes rulers (Daniel 2:21).
- He has a plan for His people and will carry it out (Ephesians 1:5, 11).
- He chose His people to save and purify them (2 Thessalonians 2:13).
- He is the only Sovereign (1 Timothy 1:17, 6:15).

Because God is holy...
I will devote myself to Him in purity, worship, and service.

> *"So, obey God because you are His children. Don't slip back into your old ways of doing evil; you didn't know any better then. But now you must be holy in everything you do, just as God—who chose you to be His children—is holy. For He Himself has said, "You must be holy because I am holy"* (1 Peter 1:14–16).

- God guards His holy reputation (Ezekiel 36:21–23).
- God's holiness demands exclusive worship (Joshua 24:19).
- He disciplines believers to impart His holiness to them (Hebrews 12:10).
- His holiness is unique (Exodus 15:11).
- His holiness is the standard for believers' behavior (Leviticus 19:2; 1 Peter 1:15–16).
- His holy presence rejects impurity (Isaiah 6:3–5).
- No one else is holy like He is (1 Samuel 2:2).
- The most holy One deserves constant honor (Revelation 4:8).

Because God is absolute truth...

I will believe what He says and live accordingly.

> *"You are truly My disciples if you keep obeying My teachings. And you will know the truth, and the truth will set you free"* (John 8:31–32).

- Believers know that God is true (John 3:33).
- Eternal life is knowing the only true God (John 17:3).
- Even if all humanity lies, God remains true (Romans 3:4).
- God is the Truth (John 14:6).
- God follows through on His promises (Numbers 11:22–23, 31–34).
- God's words are true and completely righteous (Psalm 19:9).
- God's truth is everlasting (Psalm 117:2).
- God's word is truth (John 17:17).
- God's words are faithful and true (Revelation 21:5, 22:6).
- God's truth can be suppressed to our peril (Romans 1: 18).
- He is "the God of truth" (Psalm 31:5; Isaiah 65:16).
- God doesn't lie but keeps His word (Numbers 23:19).
- He is full of grace and truth (John 1:14).
- His Spirit guides believers into all truth (John 16:13).
- The Holy Spirit is characterized by truth in every way (John 14:17, 15:26; 1 John 5:6).
- True freedom comes from abiding in God's truth (John 8:31–32).

Because God is righteous…
I will live by His standards.

> *"Throw off your old evil nature and your former way of life, which is rotten through and through, full of lust and deception. Instead, there must be a spiritual renewal of your thoughts and attitudes. You must display a new nature because you are a*

new person, created in God's likeness—righteous, holy, and true" (Ephesians 4:22–24).

- His righteousness is absolute (Psalm 71:19).
- He rules out of righteousness (Psalm 97:2).
- He is righteous in everything He does (Psalm 145:17).
- He delights in demonstrating righteousness (Jeremiah 9:24).
- In the end, the righteous Judge will judge righteously (2 Timothy 4:8).
- People must declare humbly God alone is righteous (Exodus 9:27; 2 Chronicles 12:6).
- The Lord's name: "The L{sc}ord{xc} is our righteousness" (Jeremiah 23:6, 33:16).

Because God is just…
He will always treat me fairly.

> *"For we must all stand before Christ to be judged. We will each receive whatever we deserve for the good or evil we have done in our bodies"* (2 Corinthians 5:10).

- A day is fixed for His righteous judgment of the world (Acts 17:31).
- All sin is ultimately against a righteous God (Psalm 51:4).
- All God's ways are righteous and deserve praise (Revelation 15:3).
- God alone is the judge (James 4:12).
- God judges all people with justice (Psalm 9:7–8).
- God's law and judgments are completely righteous (Psalm 19:7–9).
- He exercises justice toward all humanity (Genesis 18:25).
- He is just in all His ways (Deuteronomy 32:4).
- God rightly judges heart, mind, and deeds (Jeremiah 17:10).
- Jesus, our righteous defender before the Father (1 John 2:1).

- The Messiah will judge all with complete justice (Isaiah 11:4–5).
- The righteous Messiah will establish a righteous people (Jeremiah 33:16).
- The righteous God justifies those who believe in Jesus (Romans 3:25–26).

Because God is love…
He is unconditionally committed to my well-being.

> *"Can anything ever separate us from Christ's love? Does it mean He no longer loves us if we have trouble or calamity, or are persecuted, or are hungry or cold or in danger or threatened with death?" "No, despite all these things, overwhelming victory is ours through Christ, who loved us. And I am convinced that nothing can ever separate us from His love, Death can't, and life can't. The angels can't, and the demons can't. Our fears for today, our worries about tomorrow, and even the powers of hell cannot keep God's love away. Whether we are high above the sky or in the deepest ocean, nothing in all creation will ever be able to separate us from the love of God that is revealed in Christ Jesus our Lord"* (Romans 8:35, 37–39).

- As a father, God corrects His beloved children (Proverbs 3:12).
- Believers should imitate God's universal love (Matthew 5:44–45).
- Eternal plans are motivated by His love (Ephesians 1:4–5).
- God loves and preserves His godly people (Psalm 37:28).
- God loves His people, even when they are faithless (Hosea 3:1).
- God deserves thanks because of His perpetual love (Psalm 100:5).

- God loved the world enough to send His Son to die (John 3:16).
- God loves those who love His Son (and obey Him) (John 14:21).
- His love is poured into believers' hearts (Romans 5:5).
- God is love, and those who know God love others (1 John 4:7–8, 20–21).
- Nothing can separate the believer from His love (Romans 8:38–39).
- To love enemies and the wicked is to be like God (Luke 6:35).

Because God is merciful…
He forgives me of my sins when I sincerely confess them.

> *"Have mercy on me, O God, because of Your unfailing love. Because of Your great compassion, blot out the stain of my sins. Create in me a clean heart, O God. Renew a right spirit within me. Do not banish me from Your presence, and don't take Your Holy Spirit from me. Restore to me again the joy of Your salvation, and make me willing to obey You"* (Psalm 51) *or "If we confess our sins to Him, He Is faithful and just to forgive us and to cleanse us from every wrong"* (1 John 1:9).

- As a father, God corrects His beloved children (Proverbs 3:12).
- Believers should imitate God's universal love (Matthew 5:44–45).
- Eternal plans are motivated by His love (Ephesians 1:4–5).
- God loves and preserves His godly people (Psalm 37:28).
- God loves His people, even when they are faithless (Hosea 3:1).
- God deserves thanks because of His perpetual love (Psalm 100:5).

- God loved the world enough to send His Son to die (John 3:16).
- God loves those who love His Son (and obey Him) (John 14:21).
- His love is poured into believers' hearts (Romans 5:5).
- God is love, and those who know God love others (1 John 4:7–8, 20–21).
- Nothing can separate the believer from His love (Romans 8:38–39).
- To love enemies and the wicked is to be like God (Luke 6:35).

Because God is faithful...
I will trust Him to always keep His promises.

> *"Remember that the temptations that come into your life are no different from what others experience. And God is faithful. He will keep the temptation from becoming so strong that you can't stand up against it. And when you are tempted, He will show you a way out so that you will not give in to it"* (1 Corinthians 10:13).

- Forgives the repentant (1 John 1:9).
- God is faithful to the faithful (Deuteronomy 7:7–11).
- God deserves thanks for His constant faithfulness (Psalm 100:5).
- God is faithful through calamity (Lamentations 3:22–23).
- God faithfully matures believers (1 Thessalonians 5:24).
- God is faithful to fulfill His promises (Hebrews 10:23).
- His faithfulness endures (Psalm 119:90).
- His faithfulness is immeasurable (Psalm 36:5).

Because God never changes…
My future is secure and eternal.

> *"Who has done such mighty deeds, directing the affairs of the human race as each new generation marches by? It is I, the LORD, the First and the Last"* (Isaiah 41:4).

- God never changes (Malachi 3:6).
- God is consistent throughout all time (Hebrews 13:8).
- God is good—all the time (James 1:17).
- He doesn't lie and is true to His word (Numbers 23:19).
- His love is never-ending (Lamentations 3:22–23).
- Though the universe will change, God never will (Psalm 102:25–27; Hebrews 1:10–12).

Appendix B
The Beatitudes
(Matthew 5:3–12)

Jesus said, "Blessed are the poor in spirit, for theirs is the kingdom of heaven. Blessed are those who mourn, for they will be comforted. Blessed are the meek, for they will inherit the earth. Blessed are those who hunger and thirst for righteousness, for they will be filled. Blessed are the merciful, for they will be shown mercy. Blessed are the pure in heart, for they will see God. Blessed are the peacemakers, for they will be called children of God. Blessed are those who are persecuted because of righteousness, for theirs is the kingdom of heaven.

"Blessed are you when people insult you, persecute you and falsely say all kinds of evil against you because of me. Rejoice and be glad, because great is your reward in heaven, for in the same way they persecuted the prophets who were before you."

APPENDIX C
The Fruit of the Spirit
(Galatians 5:22–23)

- Love:

    "Love is patient, love is kind. It does not envy, it does not boast, it is not proud. It does not dishonor others, it is not self-seeking, it is not easily angered, it keeps no record of wrongs. Love does not delight in evil but rejoices with the truth. It always protects, always trusts, always hopes, always perseveres" (1 Corinthians 13:4–7 NIV).

    "And above all things have fervent love for one another, for 'love will cover a multitude of sins'" (1 Peter 4:8).

- Joy:

    "Rejoice in the Lord always; again, I will say, rejoice" (Philippians 4:4)!

    "Rejoice always; pray without ceasing; in everything give thanks; for this is God's will for you in Christ Jesus" (1 Thessalonians 5:16–18).

"Now may the God of hope fill you with all joy and peace in believing, so that you will abound in hope by the power of the Holy Spirit" (Romans 15:13).

- Peace:

  "You will keep him in perfect peace, whose mind is stayed on You, because he trusts in You" (Isaiah 26:3 NKJV).

  "Be anxious for nothing, but in everything by prayer and supplication with thanksgiving let your requests be made known to God. And the peace of God, which surpasses all comprehension, will guard your hearts and your minds in Christ Jesus" (Philippians 4:6–7).

  "Let the peace of Christ rule in your hearts, to which indeed you were called in one body; and be thankful" (Colossians 3:15).

- Patience:

  "Rest in the LORD and wait patiently for Him; do not fret because of him who prospers in his way, because of the man who carries out wicked schemes" (Psalm 37:7).

  "Here is the patience of the saints; here are those who keep the commandments of God and the faith of Jesus" (Revelation 14:12 NKJV).

  "The Lord is not slow about His promise, as some count slowness, but is patient toward you, not wishing for any to perish but for all to come to repentance" (2 Peter 3:9).

- Kindness:

  "Be kind to one another, tender-hearted, forgiving each other, just as God in Christ also has forgiven you" (Ephesians 4:32).

  "Those who are kind benefit themselves, but the cruel bring ruin on themselves" (Proverbs 11:17 NIV).

  "Love is patient, love is kind..." (1 Corinthians 13:4).

- Goodness:

  "Surely goodness and lovingkindness will follow me all the days of my life, and I will dwell in the house of the LORD forever" (Psalm 23:6).

  "Who among you is wise and understanding? Let him show by his good behavior his deeds in the gentleness of wisdom" (James 3:13).

  "Do not remember the sins of my youth or my transgressions; according to Your lovingkindness remember me, for Your goodness' sake, O LORD" (Psalm 25:7).

- Faithfulness:

  "A faithful man will abound with blessings, but he who makes haste to be rich will not go unpunished" (Proverbs 28:20).

  "For we walk by faith, not by sight" (2 Corinthians 5:7).

"Most men will proclaim each his own goodness, but who can find a faithful man" (Proverbs 20:6 NKJV).

- Gentleness:

  "Let your gentleness be evident to all. The Lord is near" (Philippians 4:5 NIV).

  "To be peaceable, gentle, showing every consideration for all men" (Titus 3:2).

  "A gentle answer turns away wrath, but a harsh word stirs up anger" (Proverbs 15:1).

- Self-control:

  "Like a city that is broken into and without walls is a man who has no control over his spirit" (Proverbs 25:28).

  "He who is slow to anger is better than the mighty, and he who rules his spirit, than he who captures a city" (Proverbs 16:32).

  "The end of all things is near; therefore, be of sound judgment and sober spirit for the purpose of prayer" (1 Peter 4:7).

Appendix D
Coaching with a Game Plan
(St. Clair 2007)

Game plan to radically restructure your own life and mirror Jesus's way of coaching.

1. Stop now to ask why. Set aside an hour or two to evaluate in writing how you spend your time. Ask the question: Why I do what I do? Why do I struggle to invest in discipline a small group of people?

2. Reexamine Jesus's ministry model. Refocus on Jesus by reading the Gospels and asking, "How can I/we coach people like Jesus coached?" As you read, notice

- How Jesus carved out time for intimacy with His Father (see Mark 1:35; Luke 4:42).
- How Jesus prayed specifically for His disciples (see John 17:6–19).
- How Jesus recruited His disciples and gave them His vision for leadership (see Matt. 4:18–22; Luke 5:1–10).
- How Jesus invested in His disciples personally—heart-to-heart (see John 6).
- How Jesus related to nonbelievers (see Mark 2:13–17).
- How Jesus created opportunities for His disciples to minister to others like He did (see Luke 9:1–6).

3. Break through the confidence barrier. At some point, all of us wonder if we have what it takes. If you've never been disciplined, it's easy to question what right you have in discipling others. Jesus addressed this fear with an awesome promise to His disciples: "He who believes in Me, the works that I do he will do also; and greater works than these he will do, because I go to My Father" (John 14:12).

4. Find your team. Jesus pursued life-on-life mentoring with His disciples. It made all the difference in His ministry. Paul took a similar approach and it, too, led to greater effectiveness (think of Timothy, Silas, Erastus, Trophimus... the list goes on). It makes sense that if Jesus and Paul pursued mentoring and it made all the difference for them, then certainly it will make all the difference for us as well. With this in mind, who does God want you to disciple? Meet with these people one-on-one. Challenge each one to become part of your coaching team.

5. Coach your players. When we coach, we build relationships similar to the ones Jesus had with His disciples. "Mentoring is the emotional glue and is the relational glue that can hold our generation to the last and to the next. Mentoring is the relational bridge connecting, strengthening and stabilizing future generations of Christians."

6. Visualize your coaching tree. When we disciple, our lives influence more people over time than we can imagine. Picture yourself as fruit on the coaching tree of Jesus or Paul twenty-one centuries later. It's hard to even conceive of the size of that coaching tree! Now visualize what the Holy Spirit wants to do through you when you decide to refocus on doing ministry Jesus's way.

APPENDIX E
How to Acquire the Three Core Attributes that Facilitate a Global Mindset

1. Psychological Capital

Psychological capital is focused mostly around our openness to diversity, respect for others and their culture, willingness to work with people across-culture, self-efficacy, cognitive flexibility, and cultural agility.

Of the three global mindset capital, psychological capital is the most complex and most challenging to attain because it is connected to our personality traits, which we took on in the early stages of our lives.

While ethnocentrism—the belief and the tendency for people to place their race, culture, and ethnic above others is a major barrier to psychological capital development, making it difficult to achieve, especially as we get older. There are some tools that can assist would-be global leaders to facilitate the development of psychological capital.

2. Tools that Facilitate Psychological Capital

Because our personalities are unique and define who we are, there aren't many available tools that can assist in altering our personality to facilitate the development of psychological capital. To assist in the development of psychological capital, we support the use of these two tools:

- The Big Five Model of personality.
- Training and Personal Development

3. The Big Five Model of Personality

The Big Five personality traits consist of five dominant personality traits that predict many essential life outcomes. It includes our mannerisms, behavior, and preferences. In the context of psychological capital development, the Big Five assessment can assist in pointing out weaknesses, which in turn allows us to make the necessary adjustment to facilitate psychological capital development.

The Big Five personality traits measure the following:

- Extraversion: Draws energy from social interactions and assertive.
- Agreeableness: Respectful, compassionate, acceptance of others, and keeps things running smoothly.
- Conscientiousness: Details oriented, productive, and responsible.
- Neuroticism: Display intensity of negative emotions.
- Openness: Openness, or openness to experience, represents a sense of curiosity about others and the world; open to thinking and learning.

4. How Does the Big Five Model of Personality Works?

The Big Five is a self-assessment test that is based on a scoring metric of "high to low." The assessment analyzes your response to a series of about fifty or so statements or phrases depending on the version. Based on your response to the statements or phrases, your result will indicate where you need improvement—low—or where you excel—high. For example, you might score "high" on agreeableness: an indication of respectfulness, compassionate, open to new things and diverse culture, and "low" on conscientiousness: a sign of impulsiveness, less structured, and procrastinator. Wherever there is a low score, there is an indication that some corrective measures or self-adjustments, mostly likely to train oneself to rise to a level of satisfaction to facilitate psychological capital development.

5. Training and Personal Development that Helps Facilitate Psychological Capital Development

Because humans are uniquely created, we will excel at a particular task and find another task difficult to handle. Because of this, no one is likely to score "high" on each of the categories on the Big Five personality test. There will be areas where our scores are low and will need improvement in order to satisfy our psychological capital development.

6. How Can We Make Improvements in Areas of the Big Five Personality Assessment Where Our Scores Are Low?

Because personality traits are difficult to change, and there are no magic pills that can change them, we can improve on our personality by training ourselves in areas that we lack. One of the most effective ways of preparing yourself is to evaluate yourself to understand who you are—self-awareness, your strengths, and weaknesses; what makes you comfortable or uncomfortable, in what situation brings out your best or worst; and what makes you the way you are. If you are able to answer these questions about yourself genuinely, you will get to understand the impact your strengths and weaknesses have on you as well as others. With a clear understanding of yourself, you can commence training yourself to improve your weaknesses as well as strengthening your strengths.

7.   Intellectual Capital

Of the three global mindset capitals, intellectual capital deals more with learning—cognitive than with personality traits. Intellectual capital consists of our knowledge and understanding of the world around us in which we transact business. In the context of globalization, intellectual capital enables us to learn and understand the multiplicity of environmental elements—politics, regional makeup, tribal groups dynamic, business competitors, rules of engagement around culture, business policies and relations, business industry specifics knowledge, to name a few that could be a potential friend or foe in our business arena. Gaining intellectual capital depends on our mindset—openness, willingness, and the amount of commitment we put into the learning initiatives.

8.   How is Intellectual Capital Gained?

The first phase in gaining intellectual capital is based on your frame of mind or mindset. That frame of mind encompasses your willingness and openness to new learning experiences and, most importantly, your desire to take responsibility for your learning development. Bear in mind that no one can make you learn or accept something that you do not want to accept or learn something that has no interest you. In the context of intellectual capital, where learning about others and their culture—food, technologies, tribal groups, language to name a few—your development depends on your frame of mind which encompasses a 360 behavioral change on your part.

Upon taking responsibility for your development, you must recognize and acknowledge your strengths and weaknesses and engage in appropriate activities that would improve on your weaknesses. By that, the mindset in which we carry into taking on challenging situations can be the determined factor for success.

9.   The Development Mindset Cultivates Our Effort to Learn

Intellectual capital is mostly a self-driven initiative. What we are willing to learn and how much effort we put into it depends on our frame of mind or mindset—learning mindset. Learning mindset or "growth mindset" (13), as it is referred to, is the amount of effort and willingness we put in when learning something new. This frame of mind or mindset takes us out of our comfort zone and pushes us to face new challenges as they arise. To say the least, mindset matters. It stabilizes our fears and enables us to take on challenges brought upon by new learning initiatives.

While intellectual capital compels us to gain knowledge and understanding of diverse cultures, environments, people, and groups, the construct also tells us that knowledge and understanding of cultures and environments vary from location to location and from group to group.

Because culture, environment, and people are not homogenous, we cannot apply what we learned in one culture or environment to the next. For example, the knowledge and understanding gained from India's culture cannot be applied in Pakistan's culture. Indians and Pakistanis cultures are different despite their closed geographical proximity and closed resembling. To that "learning agility"—the ability to learn, adapt, and apply ourselves in a continuously changing environment—can be a crucial facilitator of intellectual capital. When our learning agility is appropriately applied, it assists us in making the appropriate transition from one culture to the next. While learning agility unlocks our adaptation proficiency, it keeps us from trying to fit everyone, especially people that live in close proximity into one group. Learning agility consists of five dimensions—mental, agility, people agility, change agility, result agility, and self-awareness—all of which are critical to the global mindset construct.

For example, people agility enables us to work with others that are different from us to solve shared problems while change agility—being inquisitive and comfortable when dealing with change—are two components that are closely related to the global mindset construct. So how do we gain learning agility? While there are thousands of explanations out there on how to achieve learning agility, let me tell you that learning isn't based on how smart you are. Learning agility is achieved through the amount of effort—mindset we carry into our learning initiative.

10. Gaining Intellectual Capital Through Practical Experience

While reading and other classroom activities are some of the most formal ways in which intellectual capital is developed, other informal means, such as living abroad, offers ample opportunities for people to gain intellectual capital through immersion in host countries. Without question, living abroad or abroad assignments are the single most developmental method used to achieve "cultural agility"—the ability to perform successfully across multiple cultures. (14) Living abroad affords practical experience with the locals, foods, trends, politics, industry regulations, governments, rules of engagement, and more especially, it heightens our ability to diversity.

Other manuals may suggest living abroad is costly and learning from other senior executives with global experience is more cost-effective. While I would agree that living abroad is expensive and learning from senior executives with global experience is no doubt excellent access, I would say there are no learning experiences than that gained from practical experience. Intricate details, such as the treatment of women, minority groups, facial expressions, handshakes, and other nonverbal cues, can only be learned from practical experience.

Learning through practical experience—living abroad or abroad assignments—are no doubt expensive and protracted, usually lasting a few years. However, gaining intellectual capital through these means is priceless and cannot be learned in a classroom or from ex-expatriate—global leaders. To that end, how can multinational organizations establish a program that espouses international assignments—living abroad?

While we can't say with certainty the "how," thus, what we do know is that leadership involvement in any initiatives concerning the organization is critical. In the context of learning from international assignments—living abroad, leadership involvement—plays a significant role. By that, everything the leader does must reflect a culture that supports the initiative, as discussed in unit 2.

A multinational organization's culture should include a structured selection process of global candidates with a support system for the candidates and families. The initiative should have a measuring system to evaluate its success. Bear in mind this maxim: "what gets measured gets managed" (15) and what is managed will be successful. That said, how do multinational organizations select its candidate for an international assignment? Because being global is a personal journey and personal transformation, not everyone is cut out to be a global leader. Bear in mind, global leadership entails a global mindset, and a global mindset encompasses personality traits, cognitive ability, and social ability. These three constructs enable us to learn and to adapt to multiple environments when need be. Candidates that are most appropriate for international assignments should be evaluated based on their reasoning abilities and learning skills abilities—personality traits, cognitive, and social abilities. Candidates can be evaluated by using a self-assessment inventory. While the Big Five assessment is an appropriate tool in this initiative, there are numerous other assessments—Selection Test for International Assignees (STIA), Self-Assessment for Global Endeavors (the SAGE), and the Overseas Assignment Inventory (OAI) that could be used as well.

References

Almaki, S. H., Silong, A. D. et al. 2016. "Understanding of the Meaning of Leadership from the Perspective of Muslim Women Academic Leaders." *Journal of Education and Social Research*, Vol. 6, No 2.

Anderson, V., Caldwell, C., Barfuss, B. 2019. "Love: The Heart of Leadership: *The Moral Obligation of Leaders.*" *Graziadio Business Review. A Peer-Reviewed Journal Advancing Business Practice.* https://gbr.pepperdine.edu/2019/08/love-the-heart-of-leadership.

Baldoni, John. 2003. *Great Communication Secrets of Great Leaders*. McGraw-Hill Publishing.

Bass, B.M. 1985. *Leadership and Performance Beyond Expectations*. New York: Free Press.

Bijur, P. 2000. "The Energy of Leadership." In William Dauphinais, Grady Means & Colin Price (eds.), Wisdom of the CEO, 167-174. New York: Wiley.

Bishop, W. H. 2014. "The Necessity of Unification in Globalization: A Christian Perspective." Leadership Advance Online, Issue XXV. Regent University. www.regent.edu/lao.

———. 2013. "The role of ethics in 21st century organizations." *Journal of Business Ethics*, 118(3), 635-637. doi:http://dx.doi.org/10.1007/s10551-013-1618-1.

Bright Media Foundation. God's Attributes Listing. Retrieved from https://www.josh.org/wp-content/uploads/PDF/resources-josh_talks-attributes_of_god.pdf.

Bush, T. 2003. Theories of educational leadership and management. Sage.

Cabrera, A. and Unruh, G. 2012. *Being Global: How to Think, Act, and Lead in a Transformed World.* Boston, MA: Harvard Business Review Press.

Caligiuri, P. 2012. *Cultural agility: Building a pipeline of successful global professionals.* San Francisco, CA: Jossey-Bass.

―――. 2012. Cultural agility: Building a pipeline of successful global professionals. San Francisco, CA: Jossey-Bass.

Castillo, I., Adell, F. L., Alvarez, O. 2018. "Relationships Between Personal Values and Leadership Behaviors in Basketball Coaches." Published online Sep. 12. Doi: 10.3389/fpsyg.2018.0166. frontiers in Psychology.

Chaker, A.M., 2010. "Attack of the Rotten Tomatoes: Soil, Lighting Improvements Made Now Will Ensure a Hefty Harvest Through Fall." *Wall Street Journal,* March 10, 2010.

Ciulla, J.B. (Ed.) 2004. *Ethics: The Heart of Leadership.* Westport, CT. Praeger. ISBN-10: 0275982521; ISBN-13: 978-0275982522.

Collins. K. S. "For Effective Communication, Listen to God's Communication to Man." *The Christian Science Journal.* March 2019 Issue. Retrieved from https://journal.christianscience.com/shared/view/fuqenb886o.

Crane, T. G. 2007. *The Heart of Coaching: Using Transformational Coaching to Create a High-Performance Coaching culture.* San Diego, CA: FTA Press, a division of Crane Business Group.

Craig, E. 2000. *Concise Routledge Encyclopedia of Philosophy.* New York: Routledge.

Crippen, C. 2005. "The democratic school: First to serve, then to lead." *Canadian Journal of Educational Administration and Policy,* 47(5), 1-17.

Cristian, S., and Raluca, I. O. 2010. "Beyond the borders of globalization EU-Africa, economy and conflict." *Annales Universitatis Apulensis : Series Oeconomica, 12*(2), 589-593. Retrieved from http://0-search.proquest.com.library.regent.edu/docview/856208449?accountid=13479.

Culbertson, H. (2017). "Did the Apostle Paul Believe in the Great Commission?" http://home.snu.edu/~hculbert/paul.htm.

Dahl, R. 1957. "The concept of power." *Behavior. Sci.,* 2, 201–215.

Day D. V., Dragoni L. 2015. "Leadership development: an outcome-oriented review based on time and levels of analyses." *Annu. Rev. Organ. Psychol. Organ. Behav.* 2 133–156. 10.1146/annurev-orgpsych-032414-111328.

Drake, H. 2016. "The Emperor as a Man of God: The impact of Constantine the Greats. Conversion on Roman Ideas of Kingship." University of California. http://www.scielo.br/scielo.php?script=sci_arttext&pid=S0101-90742016000100304.

Duby, D. 2009. "The Greatest Commandment: The Foundation for Biblical Servant Leadership." Liberty University, School of Business. https://digitalcommons.liberty.edu/cgi/viewcontent.cgi?article=1010&context=busi_fac_pubs.

Ejimabo, N. O. 2013. "Understanding the Impact of Leadership in Nigeria: Its Reality, Challenges, And Perspectives." https://journals.sagepub.com/doi/full/10.1177/2158244013490704.

Ellwood, W. 2010. The No-nonsense guide to globalization (3rd ed.). Oxford: New internationalist Publicatins Ltd.

Engstrom, T. W. 1976. *The Making of a Christian Leader.* Grand Rapids, Michigan: Zondervan.

Fedler, K. D. 2006. *Exploring Christian Ethics: Biblical Foundations for Morality.* Louisville, Kentucky: Westminster John Knox Press.

Ford, M. E., and Tisak, M. S. 1983. "A further search for social intelligence." *Journal of Educational Psychology, 75*(2), 196–206. https://doi.org/10.1037/0022-0663.75.2.196.

Fry, L. W., Egel, E. 2017. "Spirituality Leadership: Embedding Sustainability in the Triple Bottom Line." *Graziadio Business Review—A Peer-Reviewed Journal Advancing Business Practice.* https://gbr.pepperdine.edu/2017/12/spiritual-leadership/.

Gabriel, B.A., and Mohamed, A. 2011. "Impact of Globalization." *European Business Review, 23*(1), 120–132. doi:http://dx.doi.org.ezproxy.regent.edu:2048/10.1108/09555341111098026.

Giles, S. 2016. "The Most Important Leadership Competencies, According to Leaders Around the World." Harvard Business Review. March 15, 2016 Article.

Goldsmith, M., Lyons, L. S., McArthur, S. 2012. *Coaching for Leadership: Writings on Leadership from the World's Greatest Coaches*. San Francisco, CA: John Wiley & Sons, Inc.

Graves, S.R., Addington, T.G. 2002. *Life @ Work on Leadership. Enduring Insights for Men and Women of Faith*. San Francisco, CA: Jossey-Bass.

Gray, G., Gray, D. 2013. "Business in the Bible. Kingdom Business Connection: Connecting Your Business to His Purpose." https://www.westcoastbible.org%2Fs%2Fs%2F5-Business-In-The-Bible.pdf&usg=AOvVaw3345NazHwQhplx14LvS-9x.

Green, R. 2009. "The Importance of Biblical Communication." http://www.faithlafayette.org/resources/info/the_importance_of_biblical_communication.

Hackman, M. Z., Johnson, C. E., 2013. *Leadership: A Communication Perspective*. Long Grove, IL: Waveland Press, Inc.

Hakanen, M., Hakkinen, M., and Soudnsaari, A. 2015. "Trust in building high-performing teams-conceptual approach." *EJBO Electronic Journal of Business Ethics and Organization Studies*. http://ejbo.jyu.fi/pdf/ejbo_vol20_no2_pages_43-53.pdf.

Hakanen, M., and Soudunsaari, A. 2012. "Building trust in high-performing teams." Technology Innovation Management Review, 2.6.

Hart, C. W., Johnson, M.D. 1999. "Growing the Trust Relationship." Cornell University School of Hotel Administration—The Scholarly Commons. Spring 1999 Articles and Chapters. https://scholarship.sha.cornell.edu/cgi/viewcontent.cgi?article=1426&context=articles.

Hay, A. 2002. "Trust and organisational change: An experience from manufacturing." *SA Journal of Industrial Psychology*, Vol. 28, No. 4, 43.

Holley, G. 2011, Jan. 22. "The Apostle Paul Embodies Evangelical Zeal, Doctrinal Flexibility." McClatchy *Tribune Business News* http://eres.regent.edu:2048/login?url=https://search-proquest-com.ezproxy.regent.edu/docview/846781705?accountid=13479.

House, R., Javidan, M., and Dorfman, P. W. 2001. "Project GLOBE: An Introduction." Applied Psychology: An International Review, 50(4), 489–505.

Hultman, K. 2002. *Balancing Individual and Organizational Values: Walking the Tightrope to Success.* San Francisco, CA: Jossey-Bass Books.

Javidan, M., Stahl, G. K., Brodbeck, F. and Wilderom, C. 2005. "Cross-border transfer of knowledge: Cultural lessons from project GLOBE." Academy of Management Executive, 19, 59–76.

Jayakody, T., and Gamage, P. 2015. Impact of the emotional intelligence on the transformational leadership style and leadership effectiveness: Evidence from Sri Lankan national universities.

Johnson, B. 2016. "Impact of Emotional Intelligence on Academic Achievement and Leadership." *BMH Medical Journal*, Vol. 3, No. 4.

Johnson, J. 2013. "Nicodemus: An Encounter." Boston College. https://www.ejournals.bc.edu. 5351-Article Text-10409-1-10-20131204.pdf.

Jonkman, F. 2011–2017. "The Missionary Methods of the Apostle Paul." Third Millennium Ministries: Pauline Studies. http://thirdmill.org/paul/missionary_methods.asp.

Journal of Strategic Human Resource Management, 4(1) http://0-search.proquest.com.library.regent.edu/docview/1733218748?accountid=13479.

Kadefors, Anna. 2004. "Trust in Project Relationships—Inside the Black Box." *International Journal of Project Management* 22: 175–82.

Karadagli, E. C. 2012. "The effects of globalization on firm performance in emerging markets: Evidence from emerging-7 countries." Asian Economic and Financial Review, 2(7), 858.

Kelley, R. 1998. Harvard Business Review In Praise of Followers. https://hbr.org/1988/11/in-praise-of-followers.

Keller, T. 2012. *Every Good Endeavor: Connecting Your Work to God's Work.* New York, New York: Penguin Group (USA) Inc.

Kouzes, Posner, et al. 2004. *Christian Reflections on Leadership Challenge*. San Francisco, CA: John Wiley & Sons, Inc. A Wiley Imprint.

Kouzes, J. M., and Posner, B. Z. 2012. *The Leadership Challenge: How to Make Extraordinary Things Happen in Organizations*. San Francisco, CA: Jossey-Bass A Wiley Imprint.

———. 2017. *The Leadership Challenge: How to Get Extraordinary Things Done in Organizations* (6th ed.). San Francisco, CA: Jossey-Bass.

Kouzes, J.M., Posner, B.Z., McAllister-Wilson, D., Lencioni, P., Ortberg, N., Blanchard, K. 2004. *Christian Reflections on The Leadership Challenge*. San Francisco, CA: Jossey-Bass.

Kruse, K. 2013. "What Is Leadership?" *Forbes Magazine*.

Kuhn, Thomas S. 2012. "The Structure of Scientific Revolutions: 50th Anniversary Ed." Chicago, Il: The University of Chicago Press.

Lindsley, A. 2012. "Made In the Image of God—The Basis for our Significance." Institute for Faith, Work, & Economics Article. https://tifwe.org/made-in-the-image-of-god-the-basis-for-our-significance.

Lingenfelter, S. G. 2008. *Leading Cross-Culturally: Covenant Relationships for Effective Christian Leadership*. Grand Rapids, MI: Baker Academic.

Littlejohn, S.W. and Foss, K.A. 2008. Theories of human communication, 9th ed. Thomson Wadsworth, Belmont, C.A.

Matei, L., and Vazquez-Burguete, J. L. 2012. "Permanent Study Group: Public and Nonprofit Marketing: Proceedings" (Vol. 33). Matei Lucica.

McElmore, G. 2016. "Inspirational Message: God Advised Moses Through Jethro." http://thenewjournalandguide.com/2016/07/07/inspirational-message-god-advised-moses-through-jethro.

Mendenhall, M. E. 2013. *Global Leadership: Research, Practice, and Development*. New York: Routledge.

Michelman, P. 2005. "What an Executive Coach Can Do for You." Business Research for Business Leaders—Harvard Business Vol. 9, No. 12. https://hbswk.hbs.edu/archive/what-an-executive-coach-can-do-for-you.

Minner, W. 2015. "Leading global organizations." *Journal of Management Policy and Practice*, 16(2), 122–126.

Mintrom, M., Cheng, M. 2014. "Creating cultures of excellence: Strategies and outcomes." *Cogent Education Journal,* Volume 1, 2014, Issue 1. https://www.tandfonline.com/doi/full/10.1080/2331186X.2014.934084.

NEO, B. S., CHEN, G. 2007, 2009. *Dynamic Governance: Embedding Culture, Capabilities and Change in Singapore.* Hackensack, NJ: World Scientific Publishing Co.

Northouse, P. G. 2013. *Leadership: Theory and Practices.* 6th ed. Thousand Oaks, CA: Sage Publications, Inc.

Demirtas, O. 2013. "Ethical Leadership Influence at Organization: Evidence from the Field." *Journal of Business Ethics* 126(2). DO: 10.1007/s10551-013-1950-5.

Oster, G. 1996. "Downstream from Babel: Lessons in Obedience for Contemporary Leaders." Virginia Beach, Virginia. Inner Resources for Leaders—School of Global Leadership & Entrepreneurship Regent University.

Phillips, P. 2016. "Adam in the Garden—Leadership Lesson." http://ironleader.org/an-introduction-to-iron-leadership-adams-leadership-in-the-garden.

Pope K. S. 2015. "Steps to strengthen ethics in organizations: research findings, ethics placebos, and what works." *Journal of trauma & dissociation: the official journal of the International Society for the study of Dissociation (ISSD), 16(2), 139-152.doi:10.1080/1529 9732.2015.995021.*

Ragnarsson, S., Kristjansdottir, E., Gunnarsdottir, S. 2018. "To Be Accountable While Showing Care: The Lived Experience of People in a Servant Leadership Organization." *Sage Journals.* https://journals.sagepub.com/doi/full/10.1177/2158244018801097.

Reina, D., Reina, M., Hudnut, D. 2017. "Why Trust Is Critical to Team Success." Center for Creative Leadership. https://www.ccl.org/wp-content/uploads/2017/05/why-trust-is-critical-team-success-research-report.pdf.

Rhinesmith, S. H. 1992. "Global Mindsets for Global Managers." *Training & Development,* 46(10): 63–69.

Roeh, T., 2008. This article is edited from the chapter, "It's Biblical: Equipping the Saints for Ministry," in *TransforMissional Coaching: Empowering Leaders in a Changing Ministry World* by Steven Ogne and Tim Roehl. Published by B&H Books, 2008. Reprinted and used by permission. http://enrichmentjournal. ag.org/201202/201202_028_biblical_foundations.cfm.

Rosha, A. and Lace, N. 2016. "The Scope of Coaching in the Context of organizational Change." Springer Link. https://link.springer. com/article/10.1186/s40852-016-0028-x.

Rost, J. 2008. *Followership: An outmoded concept*. In R. E. Riggio, I. Chaleff, & J. Lipman-Blumen (Eds.), The art of followership (pp. 53–64). San Francisco, CA: Jossey-Bass.

Rousseau, Denise M., Sim B. Sitkin, Ronald S. Burt, and Colin Camerer. 1998. "Not so different after all: A cross discipline view of trust." *The Academy of Management Review* 23: 393– 404. [CrossRef].

Rue, B. 2001. "Values-based leadership: Determining our personal values." Behavioral Science, 30 (4), 12–16.

Sashkin, M., Sashkin, M. G. 2003. *Leadership That Matters: The Critical Factors for Making a Difference in People's Lives and Organizations' Success*. San Francisco, CA: Berrett-Koehler Publishers, Inc.

Schein, E.H. 2010. *Organizational culture and leadership*. (4th ed.). San Francisco: Jossey-Bass.

Shcall, J. A. 1995. "Constantine's Effect on Early Christianity." *Manchester Academic Journal*. https://www.manchester.edu/ docs/default-source/academics/by-major/philosophy-and-reli- gious-studies/journal/vi1-2/4-schall.pdf?sfvrsn=acf8862_2.

Serrat O. 2017. *Moral Courage in Organizations*. In: Knowledge Solutions. Springer, Singapore.

Singh, A. 2009. "Organizational Power in Perspective. Leadership and Management in Engineering," Volume 9, Issue 4—October 2009. ASCE Library.

Sipe, J., and Frick, D. 2015. *Seven pillars of servant leadership*. New York, NY: Paulist Press.

Smith, C. 2014. "Paul and Leadership." The Briefing—Mathias media. www.mathiasmedia.com.

Stephenson, C. 2004. "Rebuilding trust: The integral role of leadership in fostering values, honesty and vision." *Ivey Business Journal (Online)*. http://eres.regent.edu:2048/login?url=https://search-proquest-com.ezproxy.regent.edu/docview/216175462?accountid=13479.

St. Clair, B. 2007. "Coaching Like Christ. Charisma Leader | Serving and empowering church leaders." https://ministrytodaymag.com/66-archives/unorganized/16153-coaching-like-christ.

Suci, S. C., Asmara, A., and Mulatsih, S. 2015. "The impact of globalization on economic growth in ASEAN." Bisnis and Birokrasi, 22(2), 79–87.

Tafvelin, S. 2013. The Transformational Leadership Process: Antecedents, Mechanisms, and Outcomes in the Social Services.

Talwar, B. 2009. "Comparative study of core values of excellence models vis-à-vis human values." *Measuring Business Excellence*, 13(4), 34–46. doi:http://0-dx.doi.org.library.regent.edu/10.1108/13683040911100677.

Tasseli, S. 2018. "Love and Organization Studies: Moving beyond the Perspective of Avoidance." *Sage Journals*. https://journals.sagepub.com/doi/10.1177/0170840617747924.

Tsai Y. 2011. "Relationship between organizational culture, leadership behavior and job satisfaction." *BMC health services research*, *11*, 98. doi:10.1186/1472-6963-11-98.

Uhl-Bien M., Arena M. 2017. "Complexity leadership." *Organ. Dynam.*46 9–20. 10.1016/j.orgdyn.2016.12.001.

van Dierendonck, D., and Patterson, K. 2015. "Compassionate love as a cornerstone of servant leadership: An integration of previous theorizing and research." *Journal of Business Ethics*, 128, 119–131. doi:10.1007/s10551-014-2085-z.

Van Paasschen, F. 2015. "Globalization from a business leader's point of view." *The Brown Journal of World Affairs*, 22(1), 175–189.

Van Velsor, E., McCauley, C. D., Ruderman, M. N. 2010. *Handbook of Leadership Development*. San Francisco, CA: Jossey-Bass A Wiley Imprint.

Walker, T. A. 2012. "A case study: Interpersonal skills for future business leaders to achieve organizational performance goals" (Order No. 3538845). Available from ABI/INFORM Collection. (1346224607). http://0-search.proquest.com.library.regent.edu/docview/1346224607?accountid=13479.

Wells, R. 2108. "Go Means Go: A Closer Look at the Great Commission." https://www.imb.org/2018/01/16/go-means-go-a-closer-look-at-the-great-commission.

Winston, B.E., Patterson, K. 2006. "An Integrative Definition of Leadership." *International Journal of Leadership Studies*, Vol. 1, Iss. 2. Regent University.

Witherington III, B., 2011. *Work: A Kingdom Perspective on Labor.* Grand Rapids, Michigan: Wm. B. Eerdmans Publishing Co.

Yukl, G. 2010. *Leadership in organizations* (7th ed.). Upper Saddle River, NJ: Pearson Education, Inc.

Zavada, J. 2019. "4 Types of Love in the Bible: Explore the meaning of Eros, Storge, Philia, and Agape." https://www.learnreligions.com/types-of-love-in-the-bible-700177.

Zeitchik, S. 2012. "10 Ways to Define Leadership." *Business News Daily.*

About the Authors

Drs. Cedric and Widza Bryant are the founders of Bryant & Bryant Institute (BBI), a center for democratizing leadership development. Their vision aroused while completing their doctorate in strategic leadership and recognizing the strong correlation between inadequate leadership and underdevelopment—poverty, marginalization—which are among the core issues in most developing countries.

Having experienced such problems while growing up in societies where poverty and marginalization lingered and still lingers, Cedric and Widza believe if formal leadership development, capacity building opportunities could reach the billions of people in those societies, their greater potentials can be unlocked to create more thriving and sustainable communities.

While the two understand the infeasibility of reaching the entire world, they believe by democratizing leadership development, capacity building, making it available and affordable to mission-focused organizations, governmental agencies, and for-profit businesses with a mission, the world over can solve some of its problems: hunger, fight diseases, reduce humanitarian crisis, and improve the socioeconomic status for many in a more creative manner.

Cedric and Widza are also the founders of the Vladimir Bryant Foundation (VBF), a center that provides safe housing, rehabilitation, and schooling for children with special needs in Port-au-Prince, Haiti. Their vision came after moving to Haiti from the USA and finding no systems in place for their son, Vladimir, who was diagnosed with cerebral palsy shortly after his birth. Consequently, they met many other children with disabilities, some discarded facing similar circumstances as their son. Out of these challenges, the two were compelled to create the foundation in 2011. Today, the center has evolved to include schooling, physical, occupational, and speech therapy with volunteer therapists working alongside the local staff to support and rehabilitate the children.

Drs. Cedric and Widza have been married for twenty years, and together, they have five children (two sets of twins). The two are inseparable and are very competitive. They first met while completing their bachelor of art degrees at Rider University. They continued their studies together and attended Cairn University and graduated with master's in business administration and organizational leadership, respectively. In 2016, the couple embarked on what they explain as a life-changing decision to acquire their doctorate degrees. They applied and were accepted as doctorate students from Regent University. The two finished their degrees together in strategic leadership with concentrations on global consulting and coaching.

Their love for God and commitment to the Gospel has propelled them to combine their efforts—combining their doctorate projects into one to bring forth what they believe is God's original intent for leaders—a global, accessible, and inclusive approach.

CPSIA information can be obtained
at www.ICGtesting.com
Printed in the USA
LVHW032325220421
685284LV00005B/94